Cupcakes

NEW HOLLAND

First published in 2007 by
New Holland Publishers (UK) Ltd
London • Cape Town • Sydney • Auckland
Text and photographs copyright © 2007
New Holland Publishers (UK) Ltd
Copyright © 2007 New Holland Publishers (UK) Ltd

Garfield House
86–88 Edgware Road
London W2 2EA
www.newhollandpublishers.com

Unit 1, 66 Gibbes Street
Chatwood
NSW 2067
Australia

80 McKenzie Street
Cape Town 8001
South Africa

218 Lake Road
Northcote
Auckland
New Zealand

ISBN 978 1 84537 783 0

Senior editor Corinne Masciocchi
Designers Glyn Bridgewater/Ian Sandom
Photography Frank Wieder
Food styling Sue McMahon
Production Marion Storz
Editorial direction Rosemary Wilkinson

Reproduction by Pica Digital Pte Ltd, Singapore
Printed and bound by Tien Wah Press (Pte) Ltd, Malaysia

1 3 5 7 9 10 8 6 4 2

cupcakes

SUE McMAHON

I would like to dedicate this book to my mother, Peggy McMahon, who has always encouraged me to make and decorate cakes from when I was very young. She has shared her love and enthusiasm of baking with me, and I hope that readers of this book will now enjoy sharing those skills.

Contents

Introduction

**Cupcakes are just perfect for a simple afternoon tea
or for a stunning centrepiece at an elaborate wedding –
everyone has their own little cake, and there are
no arguments over who has the largest piece!
Baking the cupcakes in paper cases seals the sides,
and if the tops are iced completely, then the cakes are
sealed to help keep them fresh.**

Baking

Position the oven shelf slightly below the centre of the oven so that the cakes are central in the oven. It is possible to cook two trays of cakes at the same time if you double the recipe ingredients, but allow about an extra 5 minutes' cooking time and swap the position of the trays in the oven after 10 to 12 minutes so that both trays cook evenly.

Serving

If the cupcakes have a soft icing as a topping, then don't stack them directly on top of one another as the topping will get spoilt. Look for pretty tiered stands to display the cakes. Nowadays you can find stands that are specifically made to hold regular-size cupcakes!

Storing

Cupcakes should be stored in an airtight container to keep them fresh. Unless they contain fresh cream they shouldn't need refrigerating, unless the room is very warm, as chilling them tends to dry them out. Keep the cakes out of bright sunlight to avoid the icings or ganache melting.

Freezing

The basic cupcakes may be made in advance and then frozen. Allow them to defrost thoroughly in a cool place for 4 to 6 hours. If they are going to be frozen, use thicker paper cases, such as foil ones, as thinner cases will wrinkle during freezing and will peel away. Freeze cupcakes without the topping and complete their decoration once they've thawed.

EQUIPMENT
AND
INGREDIENTS

Equipment

The basic items needed are bun trays and paper cases, and the important thing is to make sure that the two match up. The idea is that the cases fit snugly inside the holes of the bun tray, and that the tray supports the cupcakes during cooking so that they hold their shape. Make sure the paper cases you use aren't smaller than the bun tray holes or you'll find that the sides of the cases open out during cooking and you'll be left with flat cupcakes! The recipes in this book are based on standard-size bun trays – but if your trays are larger, then just make fewer cakes.

Bun trays

The best type of bun trays are metal ones, as the metal conducts heat well, allowing the cupcakes to cook quickly and evenly. If you choose trays with a non-stick coating, then they will be easier to clean should any of the cake mixture overflow onto the tray during baking. Many of the non-stick trays are dishwasher safe. Whichever type you choose, make sure it's spotlessly clean before use and dry thoroughly after use so that it doesn't rust. Ceramic and silicone bun moulds are also available but the cupcakes will take slightly longer to

cook in these as the materials don't conduct the heat as well as metal. All the cupcakes in this book are baked in paper cases, but if you use silicone moulds, then cases aren't required as the cakes will come out of the silicone moulds very easily, with smooth sides and hardly any crumbs.

Paper cases

Choose good quality cases, as cheaper, thinner cases can wrinkle during cooking. If the cases are made from thin paper, then any designs on them won't show up well when the cakes are cooked.

Scales

It's important to weigh ingredients accurately and to stick to one set of measures – either metric or imperial – but don't mix the two.

Wire racks

It's important to transfer the cakes to a wire rack to cool because if they are left in the bun trays after cooking they will steam and the bottom of the paper cases may go soggy.

Piping bags

It is possible to buy re-usable piping bags, such as cloth ones, but the easiest type to use are the plastic disposable ones as they don't need cleaning out afterwards. They are made from a thickish plastic and cutting the tip off will give you a good strong hole for piping plain lines without the need to use a piping tube.

Piping tubes

The best piping tubes for fine piping are the seamless stainless steel tubes. Larger piping tubes are best for swirls of icing. Keep them in a separate box to the rest of your kitchen utensils so that the piping tips don't get damaged.

Ingredients

Butter

Butter has been recommended throughout this book, apart from the recipes using oil. If you use margarine or dairy-free fat, then make sure it is suitable for baking. In recognition of healthy eating trends many manufacturers have reduced the fat contents of margarines and spreads. This means they don't work as well for baking, so choose either butter or use a fat with a fat content of at least 70%, and preferably about 80%.

Sugar

Don't worry too much if you don't have the exact sugar stated in the recipe. You can interchange the caster, light soft brown sugar and dark soft brown sugar, although if you use the darker sugars you'll find that the cupcakes will have a more treacle-like flavour as well as producing darker cakes.

Icing sugar is used to make the toppings to give a smooth, velvety finish.

Flour

Most recipes call for self-raising flour. Choose a good quality flour to help ensure that the cupcakes will rise properly. Better quality flours tend to be whiter in colour than the cheaper ones. Alternatively, a plain flour may be used with baking powder added to it. Follow guidelines on baking powder packaging to work out how much to add.

Eggs

All eggs used are medium size, unless otherwise stated. Ensure that the eggs are as fresh as possible and use them at room temperature. Recipes that use raw eggs are not suitable for pregnant women or the elderly so avoid recipes that contain raw egg white in the icing.

Sugarpaste

Use shop-bought sugarpaste. If you're unable to buy it coloured, you can colour it yourself using either paste or liquid food colourings. The easiest way to colour a batch of sugarpaste is to break off a small piece of sugarpaste and colour it to a very strong colour, then knead it into the larger piece. The colour will work in more easily if done in two stages rather than trying to colour all of the paste in one go.

Sprinkling decorations

Look out for edible sprinkling decorations in cake decorating stores. There are many different types, including coloured sugars, sugar strands and chocolate flavoured ones. Specialist stores will also sell glittery sprinkles. Be sure to keep them in a dry place and out of bright sunlight, or they will fade.

BASIC
RECIPES

Plain cupcakes

This is the simple basic recipe that is the base for many of the decorated cupcakes in the book.

Makes 12 standard-size cupcakes or use half the quantities to make 18 to 24 mini cupcakes

- 125 g (4¹/₂ oz) butter, softened
- 125 g (4¹/₂ oz) caster sugar
- 2 medium eggs
- 125 g (4¹/₂ oz) self-raising flour
- 2 Tbsp milk

- *12- or 24-hole bun tray lined with paper cases*

1 Preheat the oven to 190° C/375° F (gas 5).

2 Beat together the butter and sugar in a bowl until light and fluffy. Add the eggs, flour and milk to the bowl and beat until the mixture is smooth. Divide the mixture between the paper cases and bake in the centre of the oven until the cakes have risen and are just firm to the touch in the centre. The standard-size cakes will take about 12 to 15 minutes and the mini cakes will take 10 to 12 minutes.

3 Remove the cakes from the oven and transfer them to a wire rack to cool.

Chocolate cupcakes

Chocolate cupcakes are always a very popular choice for children – but adults will enjoy these too!

Makes 12 standard-size cupcakes or use half the quantities to make 18 to 24 mini cupcakes

- 125 g (4¹/₂ oz) butter, softened
- 125 g (4¹/₂ oz) caster sugar
- 2 medium eggs
- 2 Tbsp milk
- 100 g (3¹/₂ oz) self-raising flour
- 3 level Tbsp cocoa

- *12- or 24-hole bun tray lined with paper cases*

1 Preheat the oven to 190° C/375° F (gas 5).

2 Beat together the butter and sugar in a bowl until light and fluffy. Add the eggs and milk, and sift over the flour and cocoa, then beat until the mixture is smooth. Divide the mixture between the paper cases and bake in the centre of the oven until the cakes have risen and are just firm to the touch in the centre. The standard-size cakes will take about 12 to 15 minutes and the mini cakes will take 10 to 12 minutes.

3 Remove the cakes from the oven and transfer them to a wire rack to cool.

Lemon cupcakes

**The lemon gives these cupcakes a fresh citrus tang,
perfect with a zingy fruity topping.**

*Makes 12 standard-size cupcakes
or use half the quantities to make
18 to 24 mini cupcakes*

- 125 g (4¹/₂ oz) butter, softened
- 125 g (4¹/₂ oz) caster sugar
- 2 medium eggs
- Finely grated rind and juice
  of 1 lemon
- 125 g (4¹/₂ oz) self-raising flour

- *12- or 24-hole bun tray lined with
  paper cases*

1 Preheat the oven to 190° C/375° F
(gas 5).

2 Beat the butter and sugar together in
a bowl until the mixture is light and
fluffy. Add the eggs, lemon rind and
juice and the flour to the bowl and
beat the mixture until smooth. Divide
the mixture between the paper cases
and bake in the centre of the oven
until the cakes have risen and are just
firm to the touch in the centre. The
standard-size cakes will take about
12 to 15 minutes and the mini cakes
will take 10 to 12 minutes.

3 Remove the cakes from the oven and
transfer them to a wire rack to cool.

Quick-mix cupcakes

These are very quick to mix as no creaming stage is required. The cupcakes will have a muffin-like texture.

Makes 12 standard-size cupcakes or 24 mini cupcakes

- 175 g (6 oz) self-raising flour
- ½ level tsp baking powder
- 75 g (2½ oz) caster sugar
- 150 ml (5 fl oz) milk
- 1 medium egg
- 2 Tbsp sunflower oil

- *12- or 24-hole bun tray lined with paper cases*

1 Preheat the oven to 200° C/400° F (gas 6).

2 Sift the flour and baking powder into a bowl and stir in the sugar. In a separate bowl, lightly beat together the milk, egg and oil and stir into the dry ingredients. Stir lightly and don't over-mix or the cakes will be tough. Divide the mixture between the paper cases and bake in the centre of the oven until the cakes are a light golden colour and spring back when lightly pressed. The standard-size cakes will take about 12 to 15 minutes and the mini cakes will take 10 to 12 minutes.

3 Remove the cakes from the oven and transfer them to a wire rack to cool.

Use soya milk instead of cow's milk to make these cupcakes dairy-free.

Vanilla buttercream

This is a quick buttercream icing to make as no cooking time is required.

Makes enough for 12 standard-size cupcakes or 24 mini cupcakes

- 175 g (6 oz) butter, softened
- 350 g (12½ oz) icing sugar
- 3 Tbsp boiling water
- Few drops of vanilla extract

1 Beat the butter in a bowl to soften it. Add the icing sugar, boiling water and vanilla extract, and beat until the icing is very smooth and pale in colour.

This buttercream is best made just before it's going to be used, but if it is made in advance, press a sheet of cling-film against the surface of the icing and cover the bowl with a damp cloth to help prevent the icing from crusting, and beat it well just before using it.

Chocolate buttercream

**Adding vanilla to this chocolate buttercream helps
to enhance the chocolate flavour.**

*Makes enough for 12 standard-size
cupcakes or 24 mini cupcakes*

- 175 g (6 oz) butter, softened
- 4 level Tbsp cocoa
- 3 Tbsp boiling water
- 350 g (12½ oz) icing sugar
- Few drops of vanilla extract

I Beat the butter in a bowl to soften
it. Tip the cocoa into a separate bowl,
add the boiling water to it and mix it
to a paste, then add it to the butter
and add the icing sugar and vanilla
extract and beat until the icing is
very smooth.

> As with the vanilla buttercream,
> this icing is best made just before
> it's going to be used, but if it is
> made in advance, press a sheet of
> cling-film against the surface of the
> icing and cover the bowl with a
> damp cloth to help prevent the
> icing from crusting, and beat it
> well just before using it.

Swiss meringue buttercream

As the sugar is dissolved in the warm egg white, this makes a very smooth buttercream.

Makes enough for 12 standard-size cupcakes or 24 mini cupcakes

- 4 medium egg whites
- 250 g (9 oz) caster sugar
- Pinch of salt
- 250 g (9 oz) unsalted butter, softened
- Few drops of vanilla extract

1 Place the egg whites, sugar and salt in a bowl over a pan of simmering water and mix together well. Stir frequently while heating to prevent the egg whites from cooking.

2 After about 5 to 10 minutes, when the mixture is warm and the sugar crystals have dissolved, remove the bowl from the heat. Whisk the meringue to full volume and until the mixture is cool.

3 Add the butter and vanilla extract to the meringue – the mixture will reduce in volume and will appear curdled. Continue to whisk until the butter emulsifies completely into the meringue and forms a smooth, light and fluffy texture.

4 This buttercream is stable for 1 to 2 days at room temperature (no higher than 15° C/59° F), otherwise it may be refrigerated for up to two weeks.

Cream cheese frosting

This basic recipe may be simply altered by using orange or lime in place of the lemon.

Makes enough for 12 standard-size cupcakes or 24 mini cupcakes

- 300 g (10½ oz) cream cheese
- Finely grated rind and juice of 1 lemon
- 3–4 Tbsp icing sugar

I Beat the cream cheese to soften it, then beat in the lemon rind and juice. Finally, beat in icing sugar to taste.

> Use full fat cream cheese as lower fat cheeses are usually softer and if used for making frostings the result may be too runny.

Chocolate ganache

**This rich and smooth ganache is best made
with a very dark chocolate.**

*Makes enough for 12 standard-size
cupcakes or 24 mini cupcakes*

- 284 ml (10 fl oz) carton
  whipping cream
- 1 level Tbsp liquid glucose
- 200 g (7 oz) plain chocolate,
  roughly chopped

1 Bring the cream to the boil in a
saucepan, then remove the pan from
the heat and stir in the liquid glucose.
Place the chopped chocolate in a
bowl and pour the cream over the
chocolate. Stir the mixture until the
chocolate melts to give a chocolate
ganache.

The ganache may be used warm
when it has thickened slightly and
is of a pouring consistency or it
may be left until it's cool enough
to be of a coating consistency to
give a glossy topping. Use a palette
knife to spread it. Alternatively, it
may be left to cool completely
and then whisked to give a lighter
texture. If it thickens too much,
it can be gently warmed.

Royal icing

This recipe produces a royal icing which will set hard and is ideal for making decorations like the piped flowers on the Spring garden cakes on pages 156–57. For a softer icing for covering cupcakes, add approximately 1 tablespoon of glycerine to each 350 g (12½ oz) of icing.

Makes enough for 12 standard-size cupcakes or 24 mini cupcakes

- 2 large egg whites
- 350–500 g (12½ oz–1 lb 2 oz) icing sugar

Royal icing will keep for up to two days. Press a sheet of cling film against the surface and cover the bowl with a damp cloth. Keep in a cool place but do not refrigerate and ensure the cloth remains damp.

1 In a bowl, lightly beat the egg whites to break them down, then gradually beat in the icing sugar, using the paddle beater rather than a whisk. Add enough icing sugar until the mixture starts to thicken, then beat using the slowest speed of an electric mixer for about 10 minutes, until the icing is light and fluffy. Adjust the consistency if necessary by either adding more icing sugar if the mixture is too runny, or a few drops of water if it's too stiff – but beat for at least 2 to 3 minutes after each addition of icing sugar.

Thick glacé icing

**This versatile icing can be used on almost any cupcake.
Add more or less water to achieve different consistencies.**

*Makes enough for 12 standard-size
cupcakes or 24 mini cupcakes*

- 250–350 g (9–12½ oz) icing sugar
- 2–4 Tbsp water
- Liquid or paste food colouring

1 Sift the icing sugar into a bowl
and gradually beat in the water,
1 tablespoon at a time, to give a thick,
smooth, glossy icing. Colour the icing
as required using either paste or liquid
food colouring, adding the colour
gradually, especially if you are uncertain
of the strength of the colouring.

2 The icing may be made up a few
minutes before it is needed. Stir the
icing regularly and place a sheet of
cling-film on the surface and keep the
bowl covered with a damp cloth to
prevent the icing from crusting over.

Liquid food colouring should
be added drop by drop. Paste
colouring should also be added
in very small quantities, using a
cocktail stick or the tip of a knife.

Satin icing

This is a thick icing which will set with a satin-like sheen. It should be used as soon as it is made as it crusts over very quickly and needs to be smoothed over the cakes while it's still warm.

Makes enough for 12 standard-size cupcakes or 24 mini cupcakes

- 45 g (1½ oz) white vegetable fat
- 4 Tbsp lemon juice
- 350 g (12½ oz) icing sugar
- Liquid food colouring, optional
- 1–2 Tbsp hot water

1 Melt the white vegetable fat in a large saucepan over a low heat. Take the pan off the heat and stir in the lemon juice and half the icing sugar. Beat the mixture well. Return the pan to the heat and simmer for about 1 minute until bubbles appear all over the surface.

2 When bubbles start to form, immediately remove the pan from the heat. Beat in the remaining icing sugar, food colouring, if using, and sufficient hot water to give a thick pouring consistency. Beat well to remove any lumps and use the icing immediately before it starts to cool and set.

3 Spoon the icing over the cakes, working quickly and spreading the icing if necessary with a palette knife dipped in hot water to give a smooth surface.

Toffee topping

Using condensed milk in this recipe gives a really rich creamy toffee. Use this topping while it's hot on desserts, too!

Makes enough for 12 standard-size cupcakes or 24 mini cupcakes

- 100 g (3½ oz) butter
- 125 g (4½ oz) condensed milk
- 50 g (2 oz) caster sugar
- 1 Tbsp golden syrup

1 Place the butter in a large bowl and melt it in the microwave for about 30 to 40 seconds. Stir in the condensed milk, sugar and golden syrup. Cook the topping in the microwave for 4 to 7 minutes on high power, stirring it at the end of every minute until it is a pale golden colour. (Alternatively, the topping can be cooked in a saucepan for 4 to 7 minutes, stirring continuously, so that it does not stick to the base of the pan.)

2 Leave the topping to cool and thicken slightly, then spread over the cupcakes using a palette knife.

The sauce may be made up to two days in advance and kept refrigerated. Warm it through gently until it is smooth before using.

Modelling chocolate

This moulding chocolate can be rolled out like sugarpaste for covering cakes, or is good for any moulded decorations like flowers or animals.

Makes enough for 12 roses and 36 leaves

- 150 g (5½ oz) golden syrup
- 300 g (10½ oz) plain chocolate, melted
- Cocoa, for dusting

1 Stir the golden syrup into the melted chocolate, until the mixture thickens. It may look like it has separated, but on chilling it will form a smooth paste. Transfer the mixture to a plastic food bag and chill until the chocolate is firm enough to handle.

2 Knead the modelling chocolate lightly before using to soften it. If it's sticky, use cocoa to stop it sticking.

3 If you have hot hands, run them under cold water to cool them down before working with the modelling chocolate.

This recipe uses plain chocolate, but for white modelling chocolate use white chocolate and if it's sticky, use a little icing sugar rather than cocoa.

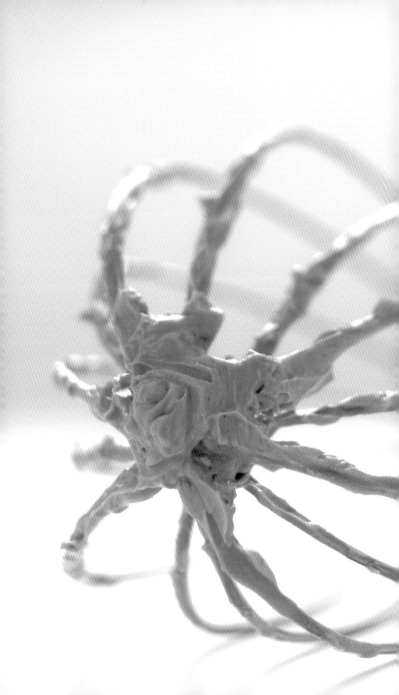

CLASSIC
COMBINATIONS

Banana and toffee

For the best flavour choose a ripe banana as bananas which are still slightly green aren't as sweet and flavourful.

Makes 12 standard-size cupcakes

For the cupcakes
- 100 g (3½ oz) butter, softened
- 100 g (3½ oz) light soft brown sugar
- 2 medium eggs
- 100 g (3½ oz) self-raising flour
- 1 ripe banana, mashed

For the topping
- 1 quantity of Toffee topping, see page 37
- 3–4 Tbsp chocolate-flavour sprinkles

- *12-hole bun tray lined with paper cases*

1 Preheat the oven to 190° C/375° F (gas 5).

2 To make the cupcakes, beat the butter and sugar together in a bowl until the mixture is light and fluffy. Add the eggs and flour to the bowl. Beat until the mixture is smooth, then fold in the mashed banana. Divide the mixture between the paper cases and bake in the centre of the oven for 12 to 15 minutes until the cakes have risen and are just firm to the touch in the centre. Remove the cakes from the oven and transfer them to a wire rack to cool.

3 For the topping, spread some toffee topping over the top of each cupcake and scatter over some chocolate-flavour sprinkles.

Mint chocolate chip

Colouring the sponge of these cupcakes green makes
them slightly unusual, but it looks great with the topping!

Makes 12 standard-size cupcakes

For the cupcakes

- 125 g (4¹/₂ oz) butter, softened
- 125 g (4¹/₂ oz) caster sugar
- 2 medium eggs
- 125g (4¹/₂ oz) self-raising flour
- Few drops of peppermint
  flavouring
- Few drops of green food
  colouring
- 100 g (3¹/₂ oz) plain chocolate
  drops

For the topping

- 1 quantity of Vanilla buttercream,
  see page 24
- Few drops of green food
  colouring
- Few drops of peppermint
  flavouring
- 3–4 Tbsp chocolate strands

- *12-hole bun tray lined with
  paper cases*

1 Preheat the oven to 190° C/375° F
(gas 5).

2 To make the cupcakes, beat the butter
and sugar together in a bowl until the
mixture is light and fluffy. Add the eggs,
flour, peppermint flavouring and green
food colouring and beat the mixture
until smooth, then stir in the chocolate
drops. Divide the mixture between
the paper cases and bake in the
centre of the oven for 12 to 15
minutes until the cakes have risen
and are just firm to the touch in
the centre. Remove the cakes from
the oven and transfer them to a wire
rack to cool.

3 For the topping, add some green
colouring to the buttercream and
flavour to taste with the peppermint
flavouring. Spread the buttercream
over the cupcakes and scatter over
the chocolate strands.

Coffee and walnut

Coffee and chicory essences also work well in this recipe as replacements for the coffee granules for both the cupcakes and the topping.

Makes 12 standard-size cupcakes

For the cupcakes
- 150 g (5¹/₂ oz) self-raising flour
- 60 g (2 oz) walnuts
- 150 g (5¹/₂ oz) butter, softened
- 150 g (5¹/₂ oz) light soft brown sugar
- 3 medium eggs
- 2 Tbsp coffee granules
- 1 Tbsp boiling water

For the topping
- 1 Tbsp coffee granules
- 1 Tbsp boiling water
- 90 g (3 oz) butter, softened
- 175 g (6 oz) icing sugar
- 12 walnut halves
- Icing sugar, for dusting

- *12-hole bun tray lined with paper cases*

1 Preheat the oven to 190° C/375° F (gas 5).

2 To make the cupcakes, tip the flour and walnuts into the bowl of a food processor and whiz until the nuts are finely ground.

3 Beat the butter and sugar in a bowl until the mixture is light and fluffy, then add the eggs, and the flour and walnut mixture. Tip the coffee granules into a small bowl, add the water and stir until the coffee has dissolved, then add to the cake ingredients in the bowl. Beat the mixture until smooth. Divide the mixture between the paper cases and bake in the centre of the oven for 15 to 20 minutes until the cakes have risen and are just firm to the touch in the centre. Remove the cakes from the oven and transfer them to a wire rack to cool.

4 To make the topping, tip the coffee granules into a mixing bowl, add the boiling water and stir until the coffee has dissolved. Add the butter to the bowl and beat until smooth, then gradually beat in the icing sugar to give a fluffy icing. Spread the icing over the top of the cupcakes and place a walnut half on the top of each. Dust with icing sugar before serving.

Strawberry 'n' cream

These taste best with fresh cream but if it's warm and you don't think the fresh cream will last, you can substitute the cream for the Swiss meringue buttercream on page 26.

Makes 12 standard-size cupcakes

For the cupcakes
- 12 standard-size Plain cupcakes, see page 18
- 6 Tbsp strawberry jam

For the topping
- 284 ml (10 fl oz) double cream
- 2 Tbsp icing sugar
- 6 medium strawberries, halved

- *12-hole bun tray lined with paper cases*

1 Cut the tops off the cupcakes and spread the cut surface with jam, then replace the tops.

2 For the topping, pour the cream into a bowl and add the icing sugar. Lightly whip the cream until it forms soft peaks, then spoon onto the top of each cupcake. Finish by pressing half a strawberry on top. Keep the cakes chilled until ready for serving.

Apple and cinnamon

The apple slices on the top look best with the skin left on, particularly if they are red-skinned apples.

Makes 12 standard-size cupcakes

For the cupcakes

- 125 g (4¹/₂ oz) butter, softened
- 125 g (4¹/₂ oz) light soft brown sugar
- 2 medium eggs
- 125 g (4¹/₂ oz) self-raising flour
- 2 level tsp ground cinnamon
- 1 dessert apple, cored and grated
- 1 dessert apple, cored and sliced

For the topping

- 4–6 Tbsp apricot glaze or sieved apricot jam
- 2 Tbsp water

- *12-hole bun tray lined with paper cases*

1 Preheat the oven to 190° C/375° F (gas 5).

2 To make the cakes, beat together the butter and sugar in a bowl until the mixture is light and fluffy. Add the eggs and then sift the flour and cinnamon together into the bowl. Beat the mixture until smooth, then stir in the grated apple. Divide the mixture between the paper cases and arrange apple slices on the top of the cakes. Bake in the centre of the oven for 12 to 15 minutes until the cakes have risen and are just firm to the touch in the centre. Remove the cakes from the oven and transfer them to a wire rack.

3 For the topping, warm the apricot glaze or jam with the water, either in a saucepan or in a microwave oven, and brush it over the top of the hot cupcakes. Serve warm or cool.

Double chocolate

These cupcakes have very rich chocolate flavours as both plain and white chocolate are used.

Makes 12 standard-size cupcakes

For the cupcakes
- 125 g (4¹/₂ oz) butter, softened
- 125 g (4¹/₂ oz) caster sugar
- 2 medium eggs
- 90 g (3 oz) self-raising flour
- 30 g (1 oz) cocoa
- 100 g (3¹/₂ oz) white chocolate drops

For the topping
- 1 quantity of Chocolate ganache, see page 30
- 60 white chocolate buttons

- *12-hole bun tray lined with paper cases*

1 Preheat the oven to 190° C/375° F (gas 5).

2 To make the cupcakes, beat the butter and sugar together until the mixture is light and fluffy. Add the eggs to the bowl, then sift the flour and cocoa over the top. Beat the mixture until smooth. Stir in the chocolate drops. Divide the mixture between the paper cases and bake in the centre of the oven for 12 to 15 minutes until the cakes have risen and are just firm to the touch in the centre. Remove the cakes from the oven and transfer them to a wire rack to cool.

3 For the topping, spread the ganache over the top of the cupcakes and decorate each cake with five white chocolate buttons.

Black forest

These cupcakes are based on the classic cake originating in the Black Forest region in Germany.

Makes 12 standard-size cupcakes

For the syrup
- 150 ml (5 fl oz) water
- 60 g (2 oz) caster sugar
- 3 Tbsp kirsch

For the cupcakes
- 12 Chocolate cupcakes, see page 20
- 6 level Tbsp black cherry conserve

For the topping
- 284 ml (10 fl oz) carton double cream
- 12 fresh cherries with stalks
- 1–2 Tbsp grated plain chocolate

- *12-hole bun tray lined with paper cases*
- *Piping bag fitted with a large star piping tube*

1 To make the syrup, pour the water into a saucepan and add the sugar. Place the pan over a low heat and stir until the sugar has dissolved. Increase the heat and boil rapidly until the mixture has reduced by about half. Remove the pan from the heat and allow the syrup to cool for about 5 minutes, then stir in the kirsch.

2 Cut the top off each cupcake and reserve the tops for 'lids'. Scoop out a small amount of the cake to create a small hollow in each. Brush the warm syrup into the hollows and spoon a little of the black cherry conserve into each hollow, then replace the lids on the cake.

3 For the topping, whisk the cream until it forms soft peaks, then spoon it into the piping bag. Pipe a swirl of cream on top of each cupcake. Place a cherry on top of each and sprinkle a little grated chocolate.

Bakewell

**The Derbyshire town of Bakewell in England claims to be
where the Bakewell pudding originated from, and these
cupcakes are a twist on the classic version.**

Makes 12 standard-size cupcakes

For the cupcakes

- 125 g (4½ oz) butter, softened
- 125 g (4½ oz) caster sugar
- Few drops of almond extract
- 2 medium eggs
- 2 Tbsp milk
- 100 g (3½ oz) self-raising flour
- 30 g (1 oz) ground almonds
- 2–3 Tbsp flaked almonds

For the topping

- 5–6 Tbsp raspberry jam
- Icing sugar, for dusting

- *12-hole bun tray lined with
  paper cases*

1 Preheat the oven to 190°C/375° F
(gas 5).

2 To make the cupcakes, beat the butter,
sugar and almond extract together in
a bowl until the mixture is light and
fluffy. Add the eggs, milk, flour and
ground almonds and beat until the
mixture is smooth. Divide the mixture
between the paper cases. Scatter the
flaked almonds for the topping over
the top of each and press them
down slightly in to the mixture.

3 Bake in the centre of the oven for
12 to 15 minutes until the cakes have
risen and are just firm to the touch in
the centre and the almonds are a light
golden colour. Remove the cakes from
the oven and transfer them to a wire
rack to cool.

4 Slice the tops off the cakes, spread
with the jam, then replace the tops.
Dust with icing sugar before serving.

Carrot and raisin

**Decorating these cakes with a sugar carrot makes it clear
what flavour they are, but as an alternative, you can scatter
over some chopped nuts. These carrots are homemade
but ready-made sugar or marzipan carrots may be
bought from cake decorating supply stores.**

Makes 12 standard-size cupcakes

For the cupcakes
- 150 g (5½ oz) self-raising flour
- ½ level tsp baking powder
- 1 level tsp ground mixed spice
- 60 g (2 oz) light soft brown sugar
- 1 carrot, peeled and grated
- 60 g (2 oz) raisins
- 125 ml (4 fl oz) milk
- 1 medium egg
- 2 Tbsp sunflower oil

For the topping
- 1 quantity of Cream cheese
  frosting, see page 28
- 12 sugarpaste carrots

- *12-hole bun tray lined with
  paper cases*

1 Preheat the oven to 200° C/400° F
(gas 6).

2 To make the cupcakes, sift the flour,
baking powder and mixed spice into
a bowl. Stir in the sugar, carrot and
raisins. In a separate bowl, lightly beat
together the milk, egg and oil and stir
into the flour mixture. Stir lightly and
make sure you don't over-mix or
the cakes will be tough. Divide the
mixture between the paper cases and
bake in the centre of the oven for
15 to 18 minutes until the cakes have
risen and are just firm to the touch
in the centre. Remove the cakes from
the oven and transfer them to a wire
rack to cool.

3 For the topping, spread the frosting
over the cupcakes and decorate each
one with a sugarpaste carrot.

Lemon meringue

The meringue on the top of these cakes is an Italian-style meringue, which is smoother than the traditional whisked egg white and sugar type of meringue.

Makes 12 standard-size cupcakes

For the cupcakes
- 12 Lemon cupcakes, see page 22

For the topping
- 4–6 Tbsp lemon curd

For the meringue
- 3 Tbsp water
- 175 g (6 oz) caster sugar
- 1 level Tbsp liquid glucose
- 3 large egg whites

- *12-hole bun tray lined with paper cases*
- *Large piping bag fitted with a star piping tube*

1 Preheat the oven to 190° C/375° F (gas 5).

2 Spread the lemon curd over the top of the lemon cupcakes and place them on a baking tray.

3 To make the meringue, pour the water into a smallish solid-based saucepan and add the caster sugar. Place the pan over a medium heat and stir until the sugar has dissolved. Add the liquid glucose to the pan and stir briefly until dissolved. Wash down any sugar crystals on the side of the pan with a damp pastry brush. Increase the heat and boil the mixture rapidly until it reaches 121°C/248°F, occasionally washing down the sides of the pan. Meanwhile whisk the egg whites until stiff. When the sugar has reached the correct temperature, remove the pan from heat and plunge the base of the pan into a bowl of cold water to stop the cooking process.

With the mixer running at a slow speed, gradually pour the syrup over the egg whites. Continue whisking at high speed until the mixture cools. Fill the piping bag with the meringue mixture and swirl over the lemon curd.

Bake the cakes in the centre of the oven for 2 to 3 minutes or until the meringue is a light golden colour. Remove from the oven and serve immediately or within 2 hours.

You can also cook the meringue using a heat gun. Place the cakes on a wooden board to protect the work surface. Hold the heat gun over the meringue until it reaches the desired colour.

Brownies

**To save time and to make these cupcakes less rich,
the ganache topping may be omitted and the
cupcakes just dusted with icing sugar instead.**

Makes 12 standard-size cupcakes

For the cupcakes
- 100 g (3¹/₂ oz) plain chocolate
- 125 g (4¹/₂ oz) butter, softened
- 2 medium eggs
- 150 g (5¹/₂ oz) dark soft brown sugar
- 60 g (2 oz) plain flour
- 100 g (3¹/₂ oz) toasted pecan nuts, roughly chopped

For the topping
- 1 quantity of Chocolate ganache, see page 30
- 12 pecan nuts
- Icing sugar, for dusting

- *12-hole bun tray lined with paper cases*

1 Preheat the oven to 190° C/375° F (gas 5).

2 To make the cupcakes, melt the chocolate in a bowl over a pan of hot water. Cool slightly, then whisk the butter into the chocolate.

3 In a separate bowl, lightly whisk the eggs and sugar until the mixture is slightly foamy but not too thick. Fold the egg mixture into the chocolate mixture, then fold in the sifted flour. Finally fold in the chopped nuts. Divide the mixture between the paper cases and bake in the centre of the oven for 18 to 20 minutes until the cakes have risen and are just firm to the touch in the centre. Remove the cakes from the oven and transfer them to a wire rack to cool.

4 Spread the chocolate ganache over the top of the cupcakes, top with a pecan nut and dust with icing sugar.

Blondies

A pale version of a Brownie, these cupcakes have a butterscotch-like flavour.

Makes 12 standard-size cupcakes

• For the cupcakes
- 125 g (4¹/₂ oz) soft light brown sugar
- 125 g (4¹/₂ oz) butter, softened
- 2 medium eggs
- Few drops of vanilla extract
- 125 g (4¹/₂ oz) self-raising flour

For the topping
- 100 g (3¹/₂ oz) plain chocolate drops
- 125 g (4¹/₂ oz) chopped mixed nuts

- *12 hole bun tray, lined with paper cases*

1 Preheat the oven to 190° C/375° F (gas 5).

2 Heat the sugar and butter in a pan over a gentle heat, stirring until the sugar has dissolved. Remove the pan from the heat and leave to cool slightly. Stir in the eggs, one at a time and then the vanilla extract. Fold in the flour and then divide the mixture between the paper cases.

3 For the topping, sprinkle over the chocolate drops and nuts and press lightly into the mixture. Bake in the centre of the oven for 18 to 20 minutes until the cakes have risen and are just firm to the touch in the centre. Remove the cakes from the oven and transfer them to a wire rack to cool.

Toffee apple

The caramel decorations make these cupcakes special,
but if it's humid they may go cloudy and sticky very quickly,
so only decorate the cakes just before serving.

Makes 12 standard-size cupcakes

For the cupcakes

- 90 g (3 oz) butter
- 90 g (3 oz) light soft brown sugar
- 2 medium eggs
- 90 g (3 oz) self-raising flour
- 1 small apple, peeled, cored and chopped

For the topping and decoration

- 100 ml (3½ fl oz) water
- 350 g (12½ oz) caster sugar
- 30 g (1 oz) butter

- *12-hole bun tray lined with paper cases*
- *Baking sheet lined with baking parchment*

1 Preheat the oven to 190° C/375° F (gas 5).

2 To make the cupcakes, beat the butter and sugar together until the mixture is light and fluffy. Add the eggs and flour and beat until the mixture is smooth. Stir in the chopped apple. Divide the mixture between the paper cases and bake in the centre of the oven for 12 to 15 minutes until the cakes have risen and are just firm to the touch in the centre. Remove the cakes from the oven and transfer them to a wire rack to cool.

3 For the topping and decoration, pour the water into a small saucepan and add the sugar. Place the pan over a gentle heat and stir until the sugar crystals have melted. Use a damp pastry brush to wash down any sugar crystals from the sides of the pan, then increase the heat and boil the mixture, without stirring, until the

sugar turns to a caramel colour.
Remove the pan from the heat and
leave the caramel to cool slightly.
Pour half the caramel into shapes
onto the lined baking sheet and
leave the decorations to set.

4 Gently rewarm the remaining
caramel with the butter, and
working quickly and on one
cupcake at a time, spread some of
the butter caramel over the cake,
using an oiled palette knife. Make
1 or 2 small holes in the top, then
stick in 1 or 2 caramel decorations.

Baked vanilla cheesecake

These are easier to eat with a small fork or spoon, rather than with your fingers.

Makes 12 standard-size cupcakes

For the cupcakes

- 100 g (3½ oz) digestive biscuits, crushed
- 30 g (1 oz) butter, melted
- 300 g (10½ oz) cream cheese
- 60 g (2 oz) caster sugar
- 2 medium eggs
- Few drops of vanilla extract

For the topping

- 142 ml (5 fl oz) soured cream
- 30 g (1 oz) caster sugar

- *12-hole bun tray lined with paper cases*

1 Preheat the oven to 160° C/325° F (gas 3).

2 In a bowl, mix together the crushed biscuits with the butter and divide between the paper cases. Press the mixture down firmly.

3 Beat the cream cheese to soften, then beat in the sugar, eggs and vanilla extract. Divide the mixture between the paper cases. Bake in the centre of the oven for 15 to 20 minutes, or until the centre feels set when pressed lightly.

4 For the topping, mix together the soured cream and sugar and pour it over the cheesecakes, then return them to the oven for a further 10 to 15 minutes until the topping has set.

5 Remove the cupcakes from the oven and leave them to cool in the tin. Refrigerate the cheesecakes in the bun tray, preferably overnight, before serving.

CHILDREN'S FAVOURITES

Citrus bursts

**These tangy cakes have a refreshing citrus taste.
As an alternative you could use a lime instead
of the orange to make lemon and lime cupcakes.**

Makes 12 standard-size cupcakes

For the cupcakes

- 125 g (4½ oz) butter, softened
- 125 g (4½ oz) caster sugar
- 2 medium eggs
- 125 g (4½ oz) self-raising flour
- Finely grated zest of 1 lemon and 2 Tbsp juice
- Finely grated zest of 1 orange and 2 Tbsp juice

For the topping

- 1 quantity of Thick glacé icing, see page 34
- Yellow and orange food colourings

- *12-hole bun tray lined with paper cases*
- *Small disposable piping bag*

1 Preheat the oven to 190° C/375° F (gas 5).

2 To make the cupcakes, beat the butter and sugar in a bowl until the mixture is light and fluffy. Add the eggs, flour, lemon and orange juices and beat until smooth. Stir in the lemon and orange zests. Divide the mixture between the paper cases and bake in the centre of the oven for 12 to 15 minutes until the cakes have risen and are just firm to the touch in the centre. Remove the cakes from the oven and transfer them to a wire rack to cool. Cut the tops off the cakes to level them, if necessary.

3 For the topping, colour the glacé icing yellow. Take out about 2 tablespoons of icing, colour it orange and fill the piping bag. Cut off the tip to give a small hole. Spread yellow icing over each cake, then pipe lines over it with the orange icing. Allow to set before serving.

Raspberry and white chocolate

These mini cakes are a good way to encourage children to eat fruit!

Makes 24 mini cupcakes

For the cupcakes

- 50 g (2 oz) butter, softened
- 50 g (2 oz) caster sugar
- 1 medium egg
- 50 g (2 oz) self-raising flour
- 1 Tbsp milk
- 50 g (2 oz) white chocolate, chopped

For the topping

- 100 ml (3½ fl oz) crème fraîche
- 200 g (7 oz) white chocolate, melted
- 24 raspberries

- *24-hole mini muffin tray lined with paper cases*
- *Piping bag fitted with a large, plain piping tube, optional*

1 Preheat the oven to 190° C/375° F (gas 5).

2 To make the cupcakes, beat the butter and sugar in a bowl until the mixture is light and fluffy. Add the egg, flour and milk to the bowl and beat until smooth. Fold in the chocolate. Divide the mixture between the paper cases and bake in the centre of the oven for 12 to 15 minutes until the cakes have risen and are just firm to the touch in the centre. Remove the cakes from the oven and transfer them to a wire rack to cool.

3 For the topping, stir the crème fraîche into the melted chocolate, and leave to cool and thicken slightly, if necessary. Spoon or pipe onto the cupcakes. Place a raspberry onto each cake before the chocolate topping sets.

Blueberry and maple syrup

These sticky cakes are good for children to take to school as a snack. Freezing is not recommended as the blueberries will become very soft when defrosted.

Makes 12 standard-size cupcakes

For the cupcakes
- 125 g (4½ oz) butter, softened
- 60 g (2 oz) caster sugar
- 4 Tbsp maple syrup
- 2 medium eggs
- 125 g (4½ oz) self-raising flour
- 2 Tbsp milk
- 125 g (4½ oz) blueberries

For the topping
- 3 Tbsp maple syrup

- *12-hole bun tray lined with paper cases*

1 Preheat the oven to 190° C/375° F (gas 5).

2 To make the cupcakes, beat together the butter, sugar and maple syrup in a bowl until the mixture is light and fluffy. Add the eggs, flour and milk to the bowl and beat until smooth. Stir in the blueberries. Divide the mixture between the paper cases and bake in the centre of the oven for 12 to 15 minutes until the cakes have risen and are just firm to the touch in the centre. Remove the cakes from the oven and transfer them to a wire rack to cool.

3 For the topping, brush the maple syrup over the top of the warm cupcakes to give a sticky glaze.

Chocolate and peanut butter

If you prefer a more chunky texture then use crunchy peanut butter rather than the smooth type.

Makes 12 standard-size cupcakes

For the frosting
- 200 g (7 oz) cream cheese
- 60 g (2 oz) unsalted butter, softened
- 125 g (4¹/₂ oz) smooth peanut butter
- 125 g (4¹/₂ oz) icing sugar

For the cupcakes
- 12 Chocolate cupcakes, see page 20

For the decoration
- 36 chocolate-coated peanuts

1 To make the frosting, beat the cream cheese to soften it, then add the butter and peanut butter and beat until smooth. Gradually beat in the icing sugar until the frosting is light and fluffy.

2 Spread some frosting over each cake, and decorate each with three chocolate-coated peanuts.

Rocky road

These are refrigerator cakes – so no baking required!

Makes 12 standard-size cupcakes

For the chocolate cases
• 250 g (9 oz) plain chocolate-flavour cake covering, melted

For the filling
• 100 ml (3$^1/_2$ fl oz) crème fraîche
• 200 g (7 oz) plain chocolate, melted
• 150 g (5$^1/_2$ oz) digestive biscuits, crushed
• 125 g (4$^1/_2$ oz) mini marshmallows
• 100 g (3$^1/_2$ oz) walnuts, chopped

• *12-hole bun tray lined with paper cases*

1 To make the chocolate cases, brush the inside of the paper cases with the melted chocolate-flavour cake covering. Place the paper cases in the bun tray and leave the chocolate to set in the cases. Keep brushing on layers of the chocolate-flavour cake covering until all of it is used. Chill the cases for about 10 minutes. Remove the bun tray from the fridge and take out the paper cases. Carefully peel the paper away from the chocolate cups.

2 To make the filling, stir the crème fraîche into the melted chocolate, then stir in the biscuits, marshmallows and walnuts. Divide the mixture between the chocolate cups, and leave them in a cool place for at least 30 minutes until the filling has set.

Mini sticky jammy cakes

This recipe uses jam instead of sugar in the cupcakes for a very fruity flavour.

Makes 24 mini cupcakes

For the cupcakes
- 60 g (2 oz) butter, softened
- 90 g (3 oz) smooth fruit jam
- 60 g (2 oz) self-raising flour
- 1 medium egg
- 1 Tbsp milk

For the topping
- 8–10 level Tbsp smooth fruit jam

- *24-hole mini muffin tray lined with paper cases*

1 Preheat the oven to 190° C/ 375° F (gas 5).

2 Beat together the butter and jam in a bowl until the mixture is smooth. Add the flour, egg and milk to the bowl and beat the mixture well. Divide the mixture between the paper cases and bake in the centre of the oven for 12 to 15 minutes until the cakes have risen and are just firm to the touch in the centre. Remove the cakes from the oven and transfer them to a wire rack to cool.

3 For the topping, warm the jam and brush it thickly over the top of the hot cupcakes, then leave the cakes to cool completely before serving.

Use a silicone brush rather than a bristle brush so that none of the bristles come out into the jam.

Flower power

**The coloured sugar 'sprinkles' add a sparkle
to these pretty cupcakes.**

Makes 12 standard-size cupcakes

For the cupcakes
- 12 Plain cupcakes, see page 18

For the topping
- 20 marshmallows
  (10 pink and 10 white)
- Pink and lilac sugar sprinkles
- 1 quantity of Thick glacé icing,
  see page 34
- Few drops of pink and lilac
  liquid food colourings
- 12 candy-covered chocolates,
  such as Smarties or M&Ms

1 Cut each marshmallow into 3 slices,
  using scissors. Cover one cut-side of
  each of the pink marshmallows with
  pink sprinkles and use lilac sprinkles
  on the white marshmallows.

2 Colour half the glacé icing pink and
  the other half lilac. Spread the icing
  over the cupcakes. Arrange 5 slices
  of marshmallow on each cake in a
  flower-like shape, using the pink ones
  on the lilac icing and the lilac ones on
  the pink icing. Stick a candy-coated
  chocolate in the centre of each flower.

In the jungle

You can either buy ready-made animal faces, or make your own animals from sugarpaste – or for speed, you can use sweets, such as jelly snakes.

Makes 12 standard-size cupcakes

For the cupcakes
• 12 Quick-mix cupcakes, see page 23

For the topping
• Swiss meringue buttercream, see page 26
• Few drops of green liquid food colouring
• 3–4 Tbsp desiccated coconut
• 12 animals or animal faces, homemade from sugarpaste or shop-bought

I To make the topping, colour the buttercream green and spread it over the cupcakes. Add a few drops of green food colouring to the coconut and sprinkle it over the buttercream, pressing it down slightly. Place an animal decoration on top of each cupcake, sticking it in place with a little buttercream if necesssary.

Butterfly cakes

Chocolate is always a favourite with children, but as an alternative use vanilla buttercream and decorate the tops with pink sweets.

Makes 12 standard-size cupcakes

For the cupcakes
- 12 Plain cupcakes, see page 18

For the topping
- 1 quantity of Chocolate buttercream, see page 25
- Icing sugar and cocoa, for dusting
- 12 chocolate buttons

- *Piping bag fitted with a star piping tube*

1 Slice the tops off the cakes and cut the tops in half.

2 Fill the piping bag with the buttercream and pipe a swirl on top of each cake. Stick the top halves in place on top like wings. Pipe a little extra buttercream between the wings. Dust the cakes with a little icing sugar and cocoa, then press a chocolate button onto the top of each.

Crackle cakes

No cooking required! Children can help to make these, just take care when melting the chocolate.

Makes 12 standard-size cupcakes

For the cupcakes
- 200 g (7 oz) plain chocolate
- 2 Tbsp golden syrup
- 100 g (3½ oz) puffed rice cereal

For the topping
- Rainbow nonpareils (sprinkles)

12-hole bun tray lined with paper cases

I Melt the chocolate in a bowl, either in a microwave oven or over a pan of hot water. Stir in the golden syrup and then the puffed rice cereal. Divide the mixture between the paper cases. Scatter the nonpareils over the top and chill the cupcakes to set them.

Flapjacks

Moist and chewy, these make a good breakfast treat!

Makes 12 standard-size cupcakes

For the cupcakes
- 150 g (5¹/₂ oz) butter
- 150 g (5¹/₂ oz) light soft brown sugar
- 3 Tbsp golden syrup
- 275 g (9¹/₂ oz) porridge oats

For the topping
- 60 g (2 oz) plain chocolate-flavour cake covering, melted

- *12-hole bun tray lined with paper cases*
- *Small disposable piping bag*

1 Preheat the oven to 160° C/325° F (gas 3).

2 To make the cupcakes, melt the butter, sugar and golden syrup in a small saucepan. Stir the oats into the melted mixture and mix well. Spoon the mixture into the paper cases and press it down firmly. Bake the cupcakes in the centre of the oven for 15 to 20 minutes, or until the mixture is bubbling and is a pale golden colour. Remove the cakes from the oven and transfer them to a wire rack to cool.

3 For the topping, spoon the melted chocolate into the piping bag and cut off the tip to give a small hole. Pipe random lines of chocolate over the cupcakes. Leave in a cool place for the chocolate to set before serving.

Pretty 'n' pink

These are cute for any little girls!

Makes 24 mini cupcakes

For the cupcakes
• 24 Plain mini cupcakes,
  see page 18

For the topping
• 4 Tbsp smooth strawberry jam
• 1 quantity of Swiss meringue
  buttercream, see page 26
• Pink food colouring
• Pink nonpareils (sprinkles)

• *Large piping bag fitted with
  a star piping tube*

I For the topping, beat the raspberry
   jam into the buttercream. Add a
   little pink food colouring to give
   the buttercream a deeper pink colour.
   Fill the piping bag with the mixture
   and pipe a swirl onto each cupcake.
   Scatter over the nonpareils.

Chocolate rosettes

These rosettes are good for sporting events when you can give them as prizes.

Makes 12 standard-size cupcakes

For the cupcakes
- 12 Chocolate cupcakes, see page 20

For the topping
- ½ quantity of Chocolate ganache, see page 30
- 2 quantities of Modelling chocolate, see page 38 (one batch made with plain chocolate and one with white chocolate)
- Cocoa and icing sugar, for dusting

- *Fluted round cutters*
- *Cocktail sticks*

1 Spread a thin layer of ganache over the cupcakes.

2 Working on one cake at a time, roll out a small piece of dark modelling chocolate on a surface lightly dusted with cocoa and cut out a disc about the same size as the top of the cupcake. Roll around the edge with a cocktail stick to flute the disc, then place it on the cupcake. Roll out a small piece of white modelling chocolate on a surface lightly dusted with icing sugar and cut out a smaller disc. Flute the edge again and stick it over the first disc. Shape a small, flattened ball from the dark modelling paste and press it in the centre of the cake.

3 Decorate another five cakes in the same way, and then reverse the colours for the remaining six cakes.

Geometrics

**You'll need a steady hand to pipe these designs.
Be creative and pipe each cake with a different design!**

Makes 12 standard-size cupcakes

For the cupcakes
• 12 Plain cupcakes, see page 18

For the topping
• 3–4 Tbsp sieved apricot jam
• 350–500 g (12½–1 lb 2 oz) white sugarpaste
• Icing sugar, for dusting
• Royal icing, see page 32
• Paste or liquid food colourings

• *Plain round cutter*
• *Small disposable piping bags*
• *Writing piping tubes, eg No. 2, optional*

1 Spread the apricot jam over the top of the cupcakes. Roll the sugarpaste out on a surface lightly dusted with icing sugar and use the cutter to cut out discs of icing about the same size as the top of the cupcakes. Place the discs on the cakes, re-rolling the sugarpaste and cutting discs as required.

2 Colour the royal icing in your choice of colours. Either use the piping bags as they are and cut the tips off to give small holes, or for more even lines, use writing piping tubes in the bags. Pipe geometric patterns over the white sugarpaste. Leave the icing to set before serving.

Birds' nests

These cupcakes can be made at any time of year, but are
particularly good at Easter – look out for fluffy chicks to
decorate the nest if you are making them for Easter.

Makes 12 standard-size cupcakes

For the cupcakes
• 12 chocolate cupcakes,
  see page 20

For the topping
• Chocolate buttercream,
  see page 25
• 4–6 flaked chocolate bars
• 36 sugar-coated mini chocolate
  eggs

1 Spread the chocolate buttercream
over the cupcakes. Break the
chocolate bars into small pieces
and arrange them around the edges
of the cakes to make the nests. Place
three mini chocolate eggs cakes in
each nest.

GROWN-UP FAVOURITES

Caramelised banana and cinnamon

**These cakes have a crunchy topping – if you prefer
something softer, then go for the Toffee topping on page 37.**

Makes 12 standard-size cupcakes

For the cupcakes
- 90 g (3 oz) butter, softened
- 90 g (3 oz) light soft brown sugar
- 2 medium eggs
- 90 g (3 oz) self-raising flour
- 1 level tsp ground cinnamon
- 1 ripe banana, mashed

For the topping
- 6 Tbsp water
- 250 g (9 oz) caster sugar
- 30 g (1 oz) butter

- *12-hole bun tray lined with paper cases*

1 Preheat the oven to 190° C/375° F (gas 5).

2 To make the cupcakes, beat the butter and sugar together in a bowl until the mixture is light and fluffy. Add the eggs to the bowl and sift over the flour and cinnamon. Beat until the mixture is smooth, then fold in the mashed banana. Divide the mixture between the paper cases and bake in the centre of the oven for 12 to 15 minutes until the cakes have risen and are just firm to the touch in the centre. Remove the cakes from the oven and transfer them to a wire rack to cool.

3 For the topping, pour the water into a saucepan and add the sugar. Place the pan over a medium heat and stir until the sugar has dissolved. Wash down any sugar crystals from the side of the pan using a damp pastry brush. Increase the heat and boil gently, without stirring so that the mixture does not crystallise, until the sugar turns to a caramel colour. Remove the pan from the heat and add the butter and swirl it around until it's mixed in, but make sure you do not stir the mixture to help prevent crystallisation. Pour the mixture over the cakes and leave to set before serving.

Pina colada

The true cocktail in a cake!

Makes 12 standard-size cupcakes

For the cupcakes
- 90 g (3 oz) butter, softened
- 125 g (4½ oz) caster sugar
- 125 ml (4½ fl oz) coconut cream (from a carton)
- 2 medium eggs
- 2 Tbsp coconut-flavoured rum
- 150 g (5½ oz) self-raising flour
- 100 g (3½ oz) glacé pineapple, chopped

For the topping
- 300 g (10½ oz) icing sugar
- 1 Tbsp coconut-flavoured rum
- Approx 100 ml (3½ fl oz) coconut cream (from a carton)
- 12 pieces glacé pineapple
- 12 glacé or maraschino cherries

- *12-hole bun tray lined with paper cases*
- *12 cocktail umbrellas*

1 Preheat the oven to 190° C/375° F (gas 5).

2 To make the cupcakes, beat the butter and sugar together until well mixed, then add the coconut cream, eggs, rum and flour and beat until the mixture is smooth. Stir in the glacé pineapple. Divide the mixture between the paper cases and bake in the centre of the oven for 12 to 15 minutes until the cakes have risen and are just firm to the touch in the centre. Remove the cakes from the oven and transfer them to a wire rack to cool.

3 For the topping, tip the icing sugar into a bowl. Add the rum and enough coconut cream to make a thick glossy icing. Spread some of the icing over the top of each cupcake. Thread a piece of pineapple and a cherry onto each cocktail umbrella, and press one onto each cupcake. Leave the icing to set before serving.

Rum and raisin

Use a dark rum for the best flavour in these cupcakes,
white rum tends to give a more delicate flavour.

Makes 12 standard-size cupcakes

For the cupcakes
- 125 g (4½ oz) butter, softened
- 125 g (4½ oz) light soft brown sugar
- 2 medium eggs
- 125 g (4½ oz) self-raising flour
- 2 Tbsp rum
- 100 g (3½ oz) raisins

For the topping
- 250 g (9 oz) golden icing sugar
- 125 g (4½ oz) butter, softened
- 2–3 Tbsp rum
- 60 g (2 oz) chocolate-coated raisins

- *12-hole bun tray lined with paper cases*

1 Preheat the oven to 190° C/375° F (gas 5).

2 To make the cupcakes, beat the butter and sugar in a bowl until light and fluffy. Add the eggs, flour and rum, and beat the mixture until smooth. Stir in the raisins. Divide the mixture between the paper cases and bake in the centre of the oven for 12 to 15 minutes until the cakes have risen and are just firm to the touch in the centre. Remove the cakes from the oven and transfer them to a wire rack to cool.

3 For the topping, beat together the icing sugar, butter and rum to give a smooth icing. Spread the icing over the top of the cupcakes and top with the chocolate-coated raisins.

Irish coffee

**Dusting these with cocoa makes them look
like coffee in a cup!**

Makes 12 standard-size cupcakes

For the cupcakes
- 1 Tbsp instant coffee granules
- 1 Tbsp boiling water
- 150 g (5½ oz) butter, softened
- 150 g (5½ oz) light soft brown sugar
- 3 medium eggs
- 150 g (5½ oz) self-raising flour

For the topping
- 1 Tbsp instant coffee granules
- 1 Tbsp hot water
- 250 g (9 oz) icing sugar
- 125 g (4½ oz) butter, softened
- 2–3 Tbsp Irish cream liqueur
- 12 mini coffee bean chocolates
- Cocoa powder, for dusting

- *12-hole bun tray lined with paper cases*
- *Piping bag fitted with a star piping tube*

1 Preheat the oven to 190° C/375° F (gas 5).

2 To make the cupcakes, dissolve the coffee granules in the boiling water. In a bowl, beat the butter and sugar together until light and fluffy, add the eggs and flour and pour in the coffee. Beat until the mixture is smooth. Divide the mixture between the paper cases and bake in the centre of the oven for 15 to 18 minutes until the cakes have risen and are just firm to the touch in the centre. Remove the cakes from the oven and transfer them to a wire rack to cool.

3 For the topping, dissolve the coffee in the hot water in a bowl, then sift in the icing sugar and add the butter. Beat until smooth, then add the Irish cream liqueur to taste. Fill the piping bag with the icing and pipe a swirl on top of each cupcake. Top each cake with a coffee bean chocolate and dust over with a little cocoa powder.

Lavender cakes

Lavender has all sorts of health-giving properties – but make sure it is safe to eat and hasn't been sprayed with any chemicals.

Makes 12 standard-size cupcakes

For the cupcakes
- 2 level Tbsp dried lavender flowers
- 125 g (4½ oz) granulated sugar
- 125 g (4½ oz) butter, softened
- 2 medium eggs
- 125 g (4½ oz) self-raising flour

For the topping
- 175 g (6 oz) icing sugar
- 2–3 Tbsp water
- Purple or lilac food colouring
- Lavender extract, optional
- 12 sprigs fresh lavender

- *12-hole bun tray lined with paper cases*

1 Preheat the oven to 190° C/375° F (gas 5).

2 To make the cupcakes, place the lavender flowers with the sugar in the bowl of a food processor or in a blender and whiz until the flowers are finely ground. Sieve the sugar into a bowl and discard the flowers left in the sieve. Add the butter to the bowl and beat until fluffy. Add the eggs and flour and beat until smooth.

3 Divide the mixture between the paper cases and bake in the centre of the oven for 12 to 15 minutes until the cakes have risen and are just firm to the touch in the centre. Remove the cakes from the oven and transfer them to a wire rack to cool.

4 For the topping, sift the icing sugar into a bowl and add sufficient water to give a thick, glossy icing. Colour the icing to a pale shade of lavender with the food colouring.

Add lavender extract, if using. Spread the icing over the top of the cupcakes and press a sprig of lavender onto the top of each.

Cherry and coconut

For an enhanced coconut flavour, try using a coconut-flavoured rum in place of the water for the glacé icing.

Makes 12 standard-size cupcakes

For the cupcakes
- 150 g (5¹/₂ oz) butter, softened
- 150 g (5¹/₂ oz) caster sugar
- 3 medium eggs
- 125 g (4¹/₂ oz) self-raising flour
- 50 g (2 oz) desiccated coconut
- 2 Tbsp milk
- 100 g (3¹/₂ oz) glacé cherries, chopped

For the topping:
- 1 quantity of Thick glacé icing, see page 34
- 12 glacé cherries

- *12-hole bun tray lined with paper cases*

1 Preheat the oven to 190° C/375° F (gas 5).

2 To make the cupcakes, beat together the butter and sugar in a bowl. Add the eggs, flour, coconut and milk, and beat until smooth. Stir in the glacé cherries. Divide the mixture between the paper cases and bake in the centre of the oven for 15 to 18 minutes until the cakes have risen and are just firm to the touch in the centre. Remove the cakes from the oven and transfer them to a wire rack to cool.

3 For the topping, spread the glacé icing over the cakes and top each with a glacé cherry.

A quick way of decorating the cupcakes is to put the icing in a large disposable piping bag, cut off the tip, then pipe the icing onto the cakes.

Very cherry

The colour in the cherries will colour these cupcakes pink –
which are enhanced with pink icing!

Makes 12 standard-size cupcakes

For the cupcakes
- 125 g (4½ oz) butter
- 90 g (3 oz) caster sugar
- 2 medium eggs
- 125 g (4½ oz) self-raising flour
- 1 Tbsp syrup from the jar of
  maraschino cherries
- 50 g (2 oz) maraschino cherries,
  finely chopped

For the topping
- 250 g (9 oz) icing sugar
- 1 Tbsp syrup from the jar of
  maraschino cherries
- 1–2 Tbsp water
- Few drops of pink food colouring

- *12-hole bun tray lined with paper
  cases*
- *Small disposable piping bag*

1 Preheat the oven to 190° C/375° F (gas 5).

2 To make the cupcakes, beat together the butter and sugar in a bowl until the mixture is light and fluffy, then add the eggs, flour and syrup and beat the mixture until smooth. Stir in the cherries. Divide the mixture between the paper cases and bake in the centre of the oven for 15 to 18 minutes until the cakes have risen and are just firm to the touch in the centre. Remove the cakes from the oven and transfer them to a wire rack to cool.

3 To make the topping, sift the icing sugar into a bowl, and add the syrup and enough water to give a thick spreadable icing. Colour the icing pale pink, then colour about 2 tablespoons of it to a darker shade of pink and put this darker icing into the disposable piping bag. Cut off the tip of the bag to give a small hole. Working on one cake at a time, spread the pale colour over the top of the cakes. Pipe over a spiral of the darker colour. Repeat on all the cakes. Leave for the icing to set before serving.

Blueberry and cream cheese

Only put the mint leaves on these cupcakes just before serving, or they will wilt.

Makes 12 standard-size cupcakes

For the cupcakes
- 12 Lemon cupcakes, see page 22

For the topping
- 1 quantity of Cream cheese frosting, see page 28
- 150–175 g (5½–6 oz) blueberries
- 4 Tbsp blueberry jam, sieved
- 2 Tbsp water
- 12 sprigs mint

1 Spread the cream cheese frosting over the cupcakes. Arrange the blueberries on top of the cakes, pressing them into the frosting slightly to ensure they are secure.

2 Warm the jam with the water, either in a microwave oven or in a saucepan, then brush the glaze over the blueberries. Decorate with a sprig of mint on each cake.

Poppy seed and honey

**To emphasise that these cupcakes contain honey, make bee
decorations from yellow sugarpaste. Use leaf gelatine
for making wings and paint the eyes and stripes with
black food colouring.**

Makes 12 standard-size cupcakes

For the cupcakes
- 150 g (5½ oz) butter, softened
- 100 g (3½ oz) caster sugar
- 3 Tbsp clear honey
- 3 medium eggs
- 150 g (5½ oz) self-raising flour
- 2 level Tbsp poppy seeds

For the topping
- 3 Tbsp clear honey
- 3 Tbsp lemon juice
- Approx 250 g (9 oz) icing sugar
- Purple food colouring
- 12 bee decorations

- *12-hole bun tray lined with
  paper cases*

1 Preheat the oven to 190° C/375° F
(gas 5).

2 To make the cupcakes, beat together
the butter, sugar and honey in a bowl
until the mixture is light and fluffy. Add
the eggs, flour and poppy seeds, and
beat until smooth. Divide the mixture
between the paper cases and bake
in the centre of the oven for 15 to
18 minutes until the cakes have risen
and are just firm to the touch in the
centre. Remove the cakes from the
oven and transfer them to a wire rack
to cool.

3 For the topping, mix together the
honey and lemon juice. Beat in
enough icing sugar to give a thick
glossy icing. Colour the icing with the
food colouring, then spread it over
the cupcakes. Place a bee on top of
each cake. Allow to set before serving.

Pistachio

**To get a vibrant green colour for the chopped nuts
on the top of the cupcakes, rub the skins off
the nuts before chopping them.**

Makes 12 standard-size cupcakes

For the cupcakes
- 60 g (2 oz) pistachio nuts
- 125 g (4½ oz) self-raising flour
- 125 g (4½ oz) butter, softened
- 125 g (4½ oz) caster sugar
- 2 medium eggs
- 2 Tbsp milk

For the topping
- 1 quantity of Cream cheese frosting, see page 28
- 100 g (3½ oz) pistachio nuts, chopped

- *12-hole bun tray lined with paper cases*

1 Preheat the oven to 190° C/375° F (gas 5).

2 To make the cupcakes, place the pistachio nuts and flour into the bowl of a food processor, and whiz until the nuts are finely ground. Alternatively, finely chop the nuts and mix them into the flour. Beat the butter and sugar together in a bowl until light and fluffy, then add the flour mixture, eggs and milk to the bowl, and beat until smooth. Divide the mixture between the paper cases and bake in the centre of the oven for 12 to 15 minutes until the cakes have risen and are just firm to the touch in the centre. Remove the cakes from the oven and transfer them to a wire rack to cool.

3 For the topping, cover the cakes with the cream cheese frosting and scatter the chopped pistachio nuts over them.

Saffron and sultana

Saffron is often used in savoury recipes, but it's great in sweet recipes too, and it will turn these cakes bright yellow.

Makes 12 standard-size cupcakes

For the cupcakes
- Large pinch saffron strands
- 2 Tbsp boiling water
- 150 g (5½ oz) butter, softened
- 150 g (5½ oz) caster sugar
- 3 medium eggs
- 150 g (5½ oz) self-raising flour
- 100 g (3½ oz) sultanas

For the topping
- ½ quantity of Thick glacé icing, see page 34

- 12-hole bun tray lined with paper cases
- Small disposable piping bag

1 Preheat the oven to 190° C/375° F (gas 5).

2 To make the cupcakes, place the saffron strands on a piece of baking parchment and place in the oven for 1 minute to dry – take care not to leave them too long or they will burn. Remove the saffron from the oven and crumble it into a small bowl and pour over the water. Leave the saffron to steep for at least 20 minutes. In a bowl, beat together the butter and sugar until the mixture is light and fluffy. Add the steeped saffron and liquid, eggs and flour and beat the mixture until smooth, then stir in the sultanas. Divide the mixture between the paper cases and bake in the centre of the oven for 12 to 15 minutes until the cakes have risen and are just firm to the touch in the centre. Remove the cakes from the oven and transfer them to a wire rack to cool.

3 For the topping, fill the piping bag with the icing and cut off the tip of the bag to give a small hole. Pipe squiggles over the top of each cupcake and leave the icing to set before serving.

Marbled chocolate cakes

If you want to be even more creative you can make Neapolitan cakes by dividing the mixture into three and having a pink swirl too!

Makes 12 standard-size cupcakes

For the cupcakes
- 150 g (5½ oz) butter, softened
- 150 g (5½ oz) caster sugar
- 3 medium eggs
- 150 g (5½ oz) self-raising flour
- 2 level Tbsp cocoa
- 2 Tbsp milk

For the topping
- 1 quantity of Chocolate ganache, see page 30
- White chocolate curls, or grated white chocolate

- *12-hole bun tray lined with paper cases*

1 Preheat the oven to 190° C/375° F (gas 5).

2 To make the cupcakes, beat the butter and sugar together in a bowl until light and fluffy, then add the eggs and flour and beat until smooth. Divide the mixture in half and place each half in separate bowls. Add the cocoa and milk to one of the bowls and beat well. Spoon equal amounts of each mixture into the paper cases and swirl around with the tip of a knife. Bake the cakes in the centre of the oven for 15 to 18 minutes, or until they have risen and are just firm to the touch in the centre. Remove the cakes from the oven and transfer them to a wire rack to cool.

3 For the topping, spread some ganache over each cupcake and decorate with chocolate curls or grated chocolate.

Earl Grey

Earl Grey isn't just for drinking, it's good in cakes too, and it's a good partner for chocolate!

Makes 12 standard-size cupcakes

For the cupcakes
- 5 Tbsp boiling water
- 3 Earl Grey tea bags
- 150 g (5½ oz) butter, softened
- 150 g (5½ oz) light soft brown sugar
- 3 medium eggs
- 150 g (5½ oz) self-raising flour

For the topping
- 1 quantity of Satin icing, see page 36

- *12-hole bun tray lined with paper cases*

1 Preheat the oven to 190° C/375° F (gas 5).

2 To make the cupcakes, pour the boiling water over the teabags and leave them to steep for about 5 minutes, then remove the teabags, squeezing the liquid out of them. In a bowl, beat the butter and sugar until the mixture is light and fluffy, then add the tea, eggs and flour and beat until smooth.

Divide the mixture between the paper cases and bake in the centre of the oven for 15 to 18 minutes until the cakes have risen and are just firm to the touch in the centre. Remove the cakes from the oven and transfer them to a wire rack to cool.

3 For the topping, spread the icing over the top of the cupcakes, working quickly before it sets.

Lemon crunch

**As the cupcakes cool, the sugar dries out to form
a delicious crunchy crust on these cakes.**

Makes 12 standard-size cupcakes

For the cupcakes
- 125 g (4^1/$_2$ oz) butter, softened
- 125 g (4^1/$_2$ oz) caster sugar
- 125 g (4^1/$_2$ oz) self-raising flour
- 2 medium eggs
- 2 Tbsp milk
- Finely grated rind of 1 lemon

For the topping
- 3–4 level Tbsp granulated sugar
- Juice of 1 lemon

- *12-hole bun tray lined with
  paper cases*

1 Preheat the oven to 190°C/375° F
(gas 5).

2 To make the cupcakes, beat the butter
and sugar together in a bowl until the
mixture is light and fluffy. Add the flour,
eggs, milk and lemon rind to the bowl,
and beat the mixture until smooth.

3 Divide the mixture between the
paper cases and bake in the centre of
the oven for 12 to 15 minutes until
the cakes have risen and are just firm
to the touch in the centre. Remove
the cakes from the oven and transfer
them to a wire rack.

4 Immediately sprinkle the sugar for the
topping over the hot cakes. Spoon
over the lemon juice and leave the
cakes to cool.

Raspberry swirls

These are like a crumbly Viennese biscuit, so take care not to make too many crumbs when eating them!

Makes 12 standard-size cupcakes

For the biscuit cupcakes
- 175 g (6 oz) unsalted butter, softened
- 60 g (2 oz) caster sugar
- 150 g (5½ oz) plain flour
- 30 g (1 oz) cornflour

For the topping
- 4–5 Tbsp raspberry jam
- Icing sugar, for dusting

- *12-hole bun tray lined with paper cases*
- *Piping bag fitted with a large star piping tube*

1 Preheat the oven to 180° C/350° F (gas 4).

2 To make the cupcakes, cream the butter and caster sugar until light and fluffy. Sift together the plain flour and cornflour, then gradually beat into the creamed mixture. Fill the piping bag with the creamed mixture and pipe into each paper case, leaving a small hole in the centre. Bake in the centre of the oven for 15 to 20 minutes, until lightly golden in colour. Remove the cakes from the oven and transfer to a wire rack to cool.

3 To finish the cakes, fill the holes in the centre with the jam. Dust with icing sugar.

> If you have time, chill the piped mixture in the paper cases before baking to help ensure it retains its shape during cooking.

Sticky orange and cardamom

These cakes are delicious eaten warm as a dessert. If liked, you can pour custard over them.

Makes 12 standard-size cupcakes

For the cupcakes
- 4 cardamom pods
- 150 g (5½ oz) butter, softened
- 150 g (5½ oz) light soft brown sugar
- 150 g (5½ oz) self-raising flour
- 3 medium eggs
- Finely grated rind and juice of 1 orange

For the syrup
- Zested rind and juice of 1 orange
- 6 Tbsp water
- 4 Tbsp caster sugar

- *12-hole bun tray lined with paper cases*

1 Preheat the oven to 190°C/375° F (gas 5).

2 Split open the cardamom pods and discard the husks. Finely grind the seeds using a pestle and mortar.

3 To make the cupcakes, beat together the butter and sugar in a bowl until it is light and fluffy. Add the flour, eggs and orange rind and juice to the bowl and beat until the mixture is smooth. Divide the mixture between the paper cases and bake in the centre of the oven for 15 to 20 minutes until the cakes have risen and are just firm to the touch in the centre. Remove the cakes from the oven and transfer them to a wire rack.

4 While the cakes are baking, make the syrup. Put the zested rind into a small saucepan with the water and simmer it for about 5 minutes until the zest has softened. Add the sugar and orange juice to the pan and simmer until the syrup has thickened slightly. Spoon some of the zested rind over the top of each warm cupcake and spoon over the remaining syrup. These cakes are good eaten warm or cold.

Rosemary and honey

**Make sure you choose fresh young sprigs of rosemary
rather than tough woody stalks.**

Makes 12 standard-size cupcakes

For the cupcakes
- 150 g (5½ oz) butter, softened
- 100 g (3½ oz) caster sugar
- 4 Tbsp clear honey
- 3 medium eggs
- 150 g (5½ oz) self-raising flour
- 1 Tbsp finely chopped fresh rosemary

For the topping
- ½ quantity of Thick glacé icing, see page 34
- Few drops of orange food colouring
- 12 sprigs rosemary

- *12-hole bun tray lined with paper cases*

1 Preheat the oven to 190° C/375° F (gas 5).

2 To make the cupcakes, beat the butter, sugar and honey together in a bowl until the mixture is light and fluffy. Add the eggs and flour to the bowl, and beat until the mixture is smooth, then stir in the chopped rosemary. Divide the mixture between the paper cases and bake in the centre of the oven for 15 to 18 minutes until the cakes have risen and are just firm to the touch in the centre. Remove the cakes from the oven and transfer them to a wire rack to cool.

3 For the topping, colour the glacé icing to a pale orange colour and drizzle it over the cupcakes. Press a sprig of rosemary onto the top of each cake before the icing sets.

Parsnip and hazelnut

Carrot cake is really popular, but few people think of using parsnips in a similar way.

Makes 12 standard-size cupcakes

For the cupcakes
- 125 g (4½ oz) butter, softened
- 125 g (4½ oz) caster sugar
- 2 medium eggs
- 125 g (4½ oz) plain flour
- 1 level tsp ground cinnamon
- 1 small parsnip, peeled and finely grated
- 100 g (3½ oz) hazelnuts, lightly roasted and chopped

For the topping
- 1 quantity of Cream cheese frosting, see page 28
- 100 g (3½ oz) hazelnuts, lightly roasted and chopped

- *12-hole bun tray lined with paper cases*

1 Preheat the oven to 190° C/375° F (gas 5).

2 To make the cupcakes, beat together the butter and sugar in a bowl until light and fluffy. Add the eggs to the bowl and sift over the flour and cinnamon. Beat the mixture until it is smooth, then stir in the parsnip and hazelnuts. Divide the mixture between the paper cases and bake in the centre of the oven for 15 to 18 minutes until the cakes have risen and are just firm to the touch in the centre. Remove the cakes from the oven and transfer them to a wire rack to cool.

3 For the topping, spread the cream cheese frosting over the cupcakes and top with the chopped hazelnuts.

Any nuts can be used in place of the hazelnuts. These cakes are also good with pistachio or pecan nuts.

Lime and chilli

**Cupcakes with a kick! Make the chillis from red and green
sugarpaste to give an indication of the special
ingredients in these cakes.**

Makes 12 standard-size cupcakes

For the cupcakes
- 150 g (5½ oz) butter, softened
- 150 g (5½ oz) caster sugar
- 3 medium eggs
- 125 g (4½ oz) self-raising flour
- 2 level Tbsp desiccated coconut
- Finely grated rind and juice
  of 1 lime
- 1 red chilli, deseeded and finely
  chopped

For the topping
- 1 quantity of Thick glacé icing,
  see page 34
- Few drops of green food
  colouring
- 12 red chillies made from
  sugarpaste

- *12-hole bun tray lined with
  paper cases*

1 Preheat the oven to 190° C/375° F
(gas 5).

2 To make the cupcakes, beat the butter
and sugar together in a bowl until light
and fluffy. Add the eggs, flour, coconut,
lime rind and juice and chilli, and beat
until smooth. Divide the mixture
between the paper cases and bake
in the centre of the oven for 15 to
18 minutes until the cakes have risen
and are just firm to the touch in the
centre. Remove the cakes from the
oven and transfer them to a wire rack
to cool.

3 For the topping, colour the icing to a
green colour and spread it over the
cakes and decorate each one with
a red sugarpaste chilli.

CELEBRATION
CUPCAKES

Rose cupcakes

Not only are these cupcakes decorated with rose petals, but they are scented with rose water, too! Make sure you use rose petals which you are certain haven't been sprayed with any harmful chemicals.

Makes 12 standard-size cupcakes

For the cupcakes
- 150 g (5½ oz) butter, softened
- 150 g (5½ oz) caster sugar
- 3 medium eggs
- 150 g (5½ oz) self-raising flour
- 2 Tbsp rose water

For the topping
- 12 rose petals
- 1 egg white, lightly beaten
- 4–6 Tbsp caster sugar
- 350 g (12½ oz) icing sugar
- 3–4 Tbsp rose water
- Pink food colouring

- *12-hole bun tray, lined with paper cases*

1 Preheat the oven to 190° C/375° F (gas 5).

2 To make the cupcakes, beat together the butter and sugar in a bowl until light and fluffy. Add the eggs, flour and rose water to the bowl and beat until the mixture is smooth. Divide the mixture between the paper cases and bake in the centre of the oven for 15 to 18 minutes until the cakes have risen and are just firm to the touch in the centre. Remove the cakes from the oven and transfer them to a wire rack to cool.

3 To crystallise the rose petals, brush them with egg white and lightly sprinkle over caster sugar. Place them on a sheet of baking parchment and leave them to dry.

4 To make the icing, sift the icing sugar into a bowl and add sufficient rose water to give a thick glossy icing. Use the food colouring to colour the icing to a pale pink. Spread the icing on top of the cakes and place a crystallised rose petal on each

The rose petals have been coated with raw egg white, so should not be eaten by pregnant women, the elderly or anyone with a sensitive digestive system.

145

Spider cakes

These cakes are ideal for Halloween! Look out for spider shape sweets as an alternative to piping them.

Makes 12 standard-size cupcakes

For the cupcakes
- 12 Quick-mix cupcakes, see page 23

For the topping
- 3–4 Tbsp sieved apricot jam
- 250 g (9 oz) orange sugarpaste
- Icing sugar, for dusting
- 125 g (4½ oz) chocolate-flavour cake covering, melted

- *Round fluted cutter*
- *Small disposable piping bag*

1 If necessary, cut the tops off the cupcakes to level them. Spread the apricot jam over the top of the cakes. Roll out the orange sugarpaste on a surface lightly dusted with icing sugar and use the cutter to cut out discs of sugarpaste the same size as the top of the cake. Re-roll the sugarpaste as necessary to cover all the cakes.

2 Fill the piping bag with the melted chocolate and pipe a spider design on half the cakes, and spider webs on the other half. Leave the chocolate to set before serving.

Festive cupcakes

The dried cranberries add a seasonal touch to these spiced cakes, but currants or raisins may substituted if dried cranberries are unavailable.

Makes 12 standard-size cupcakes

For the cupcakes
- 125 g (4¹/₂ oz) butter
- 125 g (4¹/₂ oz) caster sugar
- 2 medium eggs
- 2 Tbsp milk
- 125 g (4¹/₂ oz) self-raising flour
- 1 level tsp ground mixed spice
- 100 g (3¹/₂ oz) dried cranberries

For the decoration
- 250 g (9 oz) white sugarpaste
- Green and red paste food colourings
- Icing sugar, for dusting
- 1 quantity of Royal icing, see page 32
- 1 Tbsp glycerine

- *12-hole bun tray lined with paper cases*
- *Holly leaf cutter*

1 Preheat the oven to 190° C/375° F (gas 5).

2 To make the cupcakes, beat together the butter and sugar in a bowl until light and fluffy. Add the eggs and milk to the bowl, sift over the flour and spice, and beat the mixture until it is smooth. Stir in the dried cranberries. Divide the mixture between the paper cases and bake in the centre of the oven for 15 to 18 minutes until the cakes have risen and are just firm to the touch in the centre. Remove the cakes from the oven and transfer them to a wire rack to cool.

3 To make the decoration, colour half the sugarpaste green and the rest red. Roll out the green on a surface lightly dusted with icing sugar. Cut out the leaf shapes using the cutter. Use the back of a small knife to mark veining on the leaves. Twist the leaves and set to one side. Make 12 leaves. Roll the

red sugarpaste into small balls to make 36 holly berries.

4 Stir the glycerine into the royal icing, then spread it onto the cakes, using a small palette knife to peak it up to look like snow. Decorate each cupcake with a holly leaf and three berries. Leave the royal icing to set before serving.

Gold chocolate

Pure gold leaf is used on these cakes for real indulgence!

Makes 12 standard-size cupcakes

For the cupcakes
- 100 g (3½ oz) butter, softened
- 100 g (3½ oz) caster sugar
- 100 g (3½ oz) plain chocolate, melted
- Few drops of vanilla extract
- 2 medium eggs, separated
- 100 g (3½ oz) plain flour

For the topping
- 4–6 level Tbsp apricot glaze or sieved apricot jam
- 1 quantity of Chocolate ganache, see page 30, at pouring consistency
- Gold leaf transfer

- *12-hole bun tray lined with paper cases*

1 Preheat the oven to 160° C/325° F (gas 3).

2 To make the cupcakes, beat together the butter and sugar in a bowl until the mixture is light and fluffy. Beat in the chocolate and vanilla extract, then beat in the yolks one at a time. Fold in the plain flour. In a separate bowl, whisk the egg whites until stiff and fold them into the chocolate mixture.

3 Divide the mixture between the paper cases and bake in the centre of the oven for 15 to 20 minutes until the cakes have risen and are just firm to the touch in the centre. Remove the cakes from the oven and transfer them to a wire rack to cool. Cut off the tops of the cakes to level them, if necessary.

4 Warm the apricot glaze and brush it over the top of the cakes. Pour the ganache over the cupcakes and leave them in a cool place to set. Press a small fleck of gold leaf on top of each cake.

Daisy fresh

Make these in bright colours for children's birthday parties or in all white for christenings or weddings.

Makes 24 mini cupcakes

For the cupcakes
- 24 Plain mini cupcakes, see page 18

For the topping
- 125–175 g (4½–6 oz) white sugarpaste
- Icing sugar, for dusting
- Paste food colourings in assorted colours
- 1 quantity of Royal icing, see page 32
- 1 Tbsp glycerine

- *Daisy cutter, e.g. Wilton Daisy Cut-Outs™*
- *Egg boxes or cupped pieces of foil*
- *Small disposable piping bag*

1 To make the daisies, divide the sugarpaste into several pieces and colour each piece a different colour. Roll out one colour on a surface lightly dusted with icing sugar and use the daisy cutter to cut out shapes. Place the flowers in a curved shape, such as an egg box or cupped piece of foil to dry. Colour a small amount of royal icing yellow, and fill the piping bag. Cut off the tip of the bag and pipe dots in the centres of the flowers.

2 Stir the glycerine into the remaining royal icing and colour it to different shades to co-ordinate with the flowers. Add sufficient water to the icing so that it will flow smoothly but is still firm enough to hold its shape. Spread icing over the tops of the cupcakes and stick a flower on top of each. Leave the icing to set before serving.

True love

To save time, you can use ready-made sugar heart decorations which are available from cake decorating supply stores.

Makes 12 standard-size cupcakes

For the cupcakes
- 12 Plain cupcakes, see page 18

For the topping
- 125 g (4½ oz) sugarpaste coloured red
- 90 g (3 oz) sugarpaste coloured pink
- Swiss meringue buttercream, see page 26

- *2 different-size heart cutters*
- *Board lined with baking parchment*
- *Piping bag fitted with a large star piping tube*

I To make the hearts, roll out the red sugarpaste on a surface lightly dusted with icing sugar. Use the larger cutter to cut out 12 hearts, re-rolling the sugarpaste as necessary. Place the hearts on a board lined with baking parchment so that they don't stick to the work surface. Roll out the pink sugarpaste and cut out 12 smaller hearts. Brush a little water onto the back of each pink heart and stick centrally on top of the red hearts. Leave the hearts to dry out, preferably overnight.

2 Fill the piping bag with the buttercream. Pipe a swirl onto the top of each cupcake and stick a heart onto each.

Spring garden

The flowers may be made several days, or even weeks in advance and stored in a cardboard box with baking parchment between the layers. Store any extra flowers in this way and as long as they are kept dry they will last for several months.

Makes 12 standard-size cupcakes

For the cupcakes
• 12 Lemon cupcakes, see page 22

For the topping
• 2 quantities of Royal icing, see page 32
• Paste or liquid food colourings
• 1 Tbsp glycerine

• *Disposable piping bags*
• *Drop flower piping tubes, e.g. Wilton 190, 1E and 2D*
• *Tray lined with baking parchment*
• *Leaf piping tube, e.g. Wilton 112*

1 Colour the royal icing as required: either make the flowers all the same colour or make them in assorted colours. Cut the tip off a piping bag and insert a drop flower piping tube. Fill the bag with royal icing and pipe flowers onto the lined tray. Do this by holding the piping bag so that the tube touches the baking parchment. Squeeze the bag and twist it slightly while squeezing the icing, then stop squeezing and lift the tube away from the flower.

2 Leave the flowers to dry. Pipe the centres of the flower in a contrasting colour royal icing, using a piping bag with the tip cut off to give a small hole. Colour some royal icing green and pipe leaves onto the baking parchment. Allow the flowers and leaves to dry, then gently peel them off the baking parchment.

Stir the glycerine into the remaining royal icing and colour as liked. Add a little water to the icing so that it looks glossy and is thick enough to be of a spreading consistency but not too runny. Spread the icing over the cakes, and place flowers and leaves on top.

Fishy wishy

A mixture of fish candles and chocolate shells give the underwater theme to these cakes – but use your imagine and you could model your own fish from sugarpaste!

Makes 12 standard-size cupcakes

For the cupcakes
• 12 Plain cupcakes, see page 18

For the shells
• Candy Colors (oil-based food colouring)
• 125 g (4½ oz) white chocolate-flavour coating

For the topping
• 1 quantity of Swiss meringue buttercream, see page 26
• Blue and green food colourings

• *Seashell moulds*
• *Fish candles*

1 To make the shells, smear some of the food colouring over the inside surface of the moulds. Melt the white chocolate-flavour coating in a bowl in a microwave oven or over a pan of hot water. Spoon the melted mixture into the moulds. Tap the moulds to knock out any air bubbles, then place the moulds in the fridge until the mixture has set. Gently tip the chocolates out of the mould.

2 Colour the buttercream for the topping using the blue and green colourings, but without mixing it in properly so that it looks marbled. Spread the buttercream over the cakes and stick the candles onto some and the chocolate shells onto others.

Chocolate roses

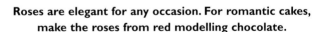

**Roses are elegant for any occasion. For romantic cakes,
make the roses from red modelling chocolate.**

Makes 12 standard-size cupcakes

For the cupcakes
- 150 g (5¹/₂ oz) butter, softened
- 150 g (5¹/₂ oz) caster sugar
- 3 medium eggs
- Finely grated zest of 1 orange
  and 2 Tbsp of juice
- 125 g (4¹/₂ oz) self-raising flour
- 2 level Tbsp cocoa

For the topping
- 1 quantity of Modelling
  chocolate, see page 38
- Cocoa, for dusting
- 250 g (9 oz) white chocolate-
  flavour cake covering coloured
  with orange candy colour, or
  Orange Candy Melts®
- 3 Tbsp crème fraîche

- *12-hole bun tray lined with
  paper cases*
- *Rose leaf cutters*

1 Preheat the oven to 190° C/375° F
(gas 5).

2 To make the cupcakes, beat together
the butter and sugar in a bowl until
light and fluffy. Add the eggs and
orange zest and juice to the bowl and
sift over the flour and cocoa and beat
until the mixture is smooth. Divide the
mixture between the paper cases and
bake in the centre of the oven for
12 to 15 minutes until the cakes have
risen and are just firm to the touch
in the centre. Remove the cakes from
the oven and transfer them to a wire
rack to cool.

3 For the rose leaves, roll out the
modelling chocolate, dusting the
surface with cocoa and cut out 36
leaves. Mark veining on the leaves
using the back of a knife and twist
the leaves slightly. Make the roses
by shaping a cone of the modelling
chocolate, then make petals from
flattened teardrop shapes and wrap

160

them around the cone. Add about six petals to each rose, then cut off the rose to give a flat base.

4 To make the topping, stir the crème fraîche into the chocolate-flavour cake covering, and if necessary leave it to cool slightly until it is of a spreadable consistency. Spread the orange topping over the cakes and stick three leaves, then a flower onto each cupcake.

Simply white

Using a textured rolling pin adds a pattern to the top of these cupcakes, but if you don't have one then you can emboss the top of the cakes using the handle of a fancy spoon.

Makes 12 standard-size cupcakes

For the cupcakes
• 12 Plain cupcakes, see page 18

For the topping
• 3–4 Tbsp apricot glaze or sieved apricot jam
• 350 g (12½ oz) white sugarpaste
• Icing sugar, for dusting
• White lustre powder colour
• 2–3 Tbsp strong clear alcohol, e.g. alcohol-based rose water or lemon extract

• *Textured rolling pin*
• *Fluted round cutter*
• *Blossom flower cutter*

1 Spread the apricot glaze over the tops of the cupcakes.

2 Roll out the sugarpaste on a surface lightly dusted with icing sugar. Roll over the surface of the sugarpaste with the textured rolling pin, pressing firmly to ensure that the design shows. Use the round fluted cutter to cut out discs to cover the tops of the cakes.

3 Re-roll the trimmings and cut out 36 blossom flowers using the blossom flower cutter. Roll a small ball of sugarpaste for the centre of each flower. Paint a little water into the centre and stick the ball of sugarpaste in place. Mix the lustre colour with the alcohol and paint over the embossed design on the cakes, and paint the centre of the flowers. Brush a little water on to the backs of the flowers and stick three onto each cake while the sugarpaste is still soft.

Starry, snowy night

The stars may be made several days in advance to ensure they are thoroughly dried out – then it's very quick to decorate these cakes.

Makes 12 standard-size cupcakes

For the cupcakes
• 12 Lemon cupcakes, see page 22

For the decoration
• 250 g (9 oz) white sugarpaste
• Icing sugar, for dusting
• Silver lustre powder colour
• 2–3 Tbsp strong clear alcohol, e.g. alcohol-based rose water or lemon extract
• Silver balls
• 1 Tbsp glycerine
• 1 quantity of Royal icing, see page 32

• *Star shape cutters*
• *Board lined with baking parchment*

1 Roll out the white sugarpaste on a surface lightly dusted with icing sugar and cut out the star shapes: 12 large stars with the centre cut out and 36 small stars. Leave the stars to dry on a board lined with baking parchment. Mix some silver lustre colour with the alcohol and paint the stars. Leave the stars on a sheet of baking parchment to dry.

2 Stir the glycerine into the royal icing and spread it over the top of the cupcakes, using a small palette knife to peak it. While the royal icing is still soft, stick one large and three small stars onto the top of the cakes, along with a few silver balls. Leave the icing to set before serving.

1 today!

These cakes may be adapted to any occasion when decorated with the appropriate numbers and candles. For example use champagne bottle candles for a 21st birthday.

Makes 12 standard-size cupcakes

For the cupcakes
- 12 Plain cupcakes, see page 18

For the topping
- 125 g (4½ oz) yellow sugarpaste
- Icing sugar, for dusting
- Blue food colouring
- 1 quantity of Swiss meringue buttercream, see page 26
- Multi-coloured fish shape sprinkles

- *Number cutters*
- *Baking parchment*
- *6 duck candles*

1 To make the numbers roll out the sugarpaste on a surface lightly dusted with icing sugar. Cut out at least six numbers using number cutters and leave them to dry on a sheet of baking parchment. Turn them over after 4 to 6 hours and leave them overnight, so they dry out completely.

2 To make the topping, colour the buttercream blue and spread it over the tops of the cupcakes. Stick numbers into the buttercream on half the cakes and scatter over the fish sprinkles. Decorate the remaining cakes with the candles.

Chocolate love

To make these cakes even more special, you can brush the hearts with edible gold lustre dust.

Makes 12 standard-size cupcakes

For the cupcakes
• 12 Chocolate cupcakes,
  see page 20

For the topping
• 100 g (3½ oz) white chocolate-
  flavour cake covering, melted
• 1 quantity of Chocolate ganache,
  see page 30

• *Small disposable piping bag*
• *Tray lined with baking parchment*

1 To make the hearts, fill the disposable piping bag with the melted chocolate and cut off the tip to give a small hole. You will need 24 heart shapes, but pipe a few extra to allow for any breakages. Leave the hearts in a cool place to set, then carefully slide a palette knife under them to release them from the paper.

2 Spread the ganache over the cupcakes and stick two hearts onto the top of each cake.

Mini birthday bows

The bows may be made several days in advance so they are ready to place on the cupcakes. The sugarpaste quantity below is enough to make a bow for each cupcake.

Makes 24 mini cupcakes

For the cupcakes
- 24 Plain mini cupcakes, see page 18

For the topping:
- 500 g (1 lb 2 oz) white sugarpaste
- Paste food colourings in pink and blue
- Icing sugar, for dusting
- 1 quantity of Thick glacé icing, see page 34

- *2 large disposable piping bags*

1 Divide the sugarpaste into two equal portions and use the paste colour to colour one half pink and the other blue. Working with one colour at a time, roll it out on a surface lightly dusted with icing sugar and cut out two long narrow strips. Fold the ends of the strips over to make loops, then criss-cross these two strips over each other to give a bow shape. Brush a little water at the join and press the pieces together. Wrap a strip around the centre as the knot of the bow. Cut off the ends to the right length to give the finished bow. Make 12 bows of each colour.

2 Colour half the glacé icing pink and the other half blue. Fill the piping bags with each colour and cut the tips off. Pipe pink icing on half the cakes and blue on the other half. Stick bows on half the cakes and leave the remaining cakes plain.

SPECIAL DIETS

Squidgy chocolate

Keep people guessing as to the secret ingredient in these cakes!

Makes 12 standard-size cupcakes

For the cupcakes
• 350 g (12$\frac{1}{2}$ lb) potatoes, peeled
• 45 g (1$\frac{1}{2}$ oz) butter
• 100 g (3$\frac{1}{2}$ oz) plain chocolate, roughly chopped
• 3 medium eggs, separated
• 60 g (2 oz) caster sugar

For the topping
• 100 ml (3$\frac{1}{2}$ fl oz) crème fraîche
• 200 g (7 oz) plain chocolate, melted
• 2–3 flaked chocolate bars

• *12-hole bun tray lined with paper cases*

1 Preheat the oven to 190° C/375° F (gas 5).

2 Cut the potatoes into chunks, place in a large saucepan and cover with water. Bring to the boil, then simmer for 15 to 20 minutes or until tender. Remove the pan from the heat and drain the potatoes. Return them to the pan, add the butter and mash well. Add the chocolate and stir until it has melted. Leave to cool.

3 In a bowl, whisk the egg yolks and sugar together, preferably using an electric mixer, until the mixture is thick and creamy and leaves a trail when the beaters are lifted. Fold into the mashed potato. In a separate bowl, whisk the egg whites until stiff, then fold into the chocolate potato mixture.

4 Divide the mixture between the paper cases and bake in the centre of the oven for 15 to 20 minutes until

the cakes have risen and are just firm
to the touch in the centre. Remove
the cakes from the oven and transfer
them to a wire rack to cool.

5 For the topping, stir the crème
fraîche into the chocolate, then
spread some onto each cupcake.
Use a sharp knife to cut each
flaked chocolate in 4 to 6 pieces
and stick a piece on each cake.

Date and banana

Use soft juicy dates, such as Medjool dates when they are available, for the best flavour.

Makes 12 standard-size cupcakes

For the cupcakes
- 125 g (4¹/₂ oz) gluten-free flour
- 30 g (1 oz) light soft brown sugar
- 125 g (4¹/₂ oz) dates, stoned and chopped
- 1 level tsp gluten-free baking powder
- 2 medium eggs
- 4 Tbsp sunflower oil
- 1 ripe banana, peeled and mashed

For the topping
- Cream cheese frosting, see page 28

- *12-hole bun tray lined with paper cases*

1 Preheat the oven to 200° C/400° F (gas 6).

2 To make the cupcakes, tip the flour and sugar into a bowl and stir in the dates and baking powder. In a separate bowl, lightly whisk the eggs and oil together and stir in the mashed banana. Stir this into the dry mixture.

3 Divide the mixture between the paper cases and bake in the centre of the oven for 15 to 20 minutes until the cakes have risen and are just firm to the touch in the centre. Remove the cakes from the oven and transfer them to a wire rack to cool.

4 For the topping, spread the cream cheese frosting over the cupcakes and texture the surface with a fork.

Currant cupcakes

The vinegar in this recipe evaporates during cooking, so the cakes don't taste at all acidic!

Makes 12 standard-size cupcakes

For the cupcakes
- 150 g (5¹/₂ oz) plain flour
- 60 g (2 oz) butter
- 200 g (7 oz) currants
- 75 g (2¹/₂ oz) cut mixed peel
- 125 g (4¹/₂ oz) soft light brown sugar
- 100 ml (3¹/₂ fl oz) milk
- ¹/₂ level tsp bicarbonate of soda
- 1¹/₂ Tbsp malt vinegar

For the topping
- ¹/₂ quantity of Thick glacé icing, see page 34

- *12-hole bun tray lined with paper cases*

1 Preheat the oven to 160° C/325° F (gas 3).

2 Sift the flour into a bowl and rub in the butter, then stir in the currants, mixed peel and sugar. Warm the milk gently in pan, then sprinkle over the bicarbonate of soda and stir in the vinegar. While it's foaming, stir it into the flour and fruit mixture.

3 Divide the mixture between the paper cases and bake in the centre of the oven for 20 to 25 minutes until the cakes have risen and are just firm to the touch in the centre. Remove the cakes from the oven and transfer them to a wire rack to cool.

4 For the topping, drizzle over the glacé icing and leave it to set before serving.

Chocolate and prune

A prune purée is used for this cakes, rather than adding butter to the recipe. The prunes also add sweetness without adding extra sugar.

Makes 12 standard-size cupcakes

For the cupcakes
- 250 g (9 oz) pitted prunes
- 300 ml (10½ fl oz) boiling water
- 1 tsp vanilla extract
- 100 g (3½ oz) self-raising flour
- 50 g (2 oz) plain chocolate, melted
- 2 medium egg whites

For the topping:
- Icing sugar, for dusting

- *12-hole bun tray lined with paper cases*

1 Preheat the oven to 180° C/350° F (gas 4).

2 Place the prunes in a bowl and pour the boiling water over them. Leave to soak for at least 30 minutes, then whiz the prunes and water in a food processor or blender until smooth. Tip the prune mixture into a bowl, add the vanilla extract and flour, then stir in the melted chocolate. In a separate bowl, whisk the egg whites until they are stiff and fold them into the prune mixture. Divide the mixture between the paper cases and bake in the centre of the oven for 20 to 25 minutes until the cakes have risen and are just firm to the touch in the centre. Remove the cakes from the oven and transfer them to a wire rack to cool.

3 For the topping, dust the cupcakes with icing sugar sifted through a fine tea-strainer.

Honey and bran

**These sticky-topped cakes make a good weekend
breakfast treat.**

Makes 12 standard-size cupcakes

For the cupcakes
- 125 g (4½ oz) self-raising flour
- 90 g (3 oz) wheat bran
- 1 level tsp baking powder
- 4 Tbsp soya milk
- 6 Tbsp runny honey
- 2 medium eggs
- 4 Tbsp sunflower oil

For the topping
- 4 Tbsp runny honey
- Juice and zest of 1 lemon
- Approx. 200 g (7 oz) icing sugar

- *12-hole bun tray lined with
  paper cases*

1 Preheat the oven to 200° C/ 400° F
(gas 6).

2 To make the cupcakes, tip the flour,
bran and baking powder into a bowl,
and mix together. In a separate bowl,
lightly beat together the soya milk,
honey, egg and oil, and stir into the
dry ingredients. Stir lightly and don't
over-mix or the cakes will be tough.
Divide the mixture between the paper
cases and bake in the centre of the
oven for 12 to 15 minutes until the
cakes have risen and are just firm to
the touch in the centre. Remove the
cakes from the oven and transfer
them to a wire rack.

3 For the topping, mix together the
honey and lemon juice and beat in
enough icing sugar to give a thick
glossy icing. Spread the icing over the
top of the cupcakes and scatter a few
strands of zested lemon rind over
each. Leave the icing to set before
serving.

Date and apple

The demerara sugar on the top of these cupcakes gives a pleasant crunch to them.

Makes 12 standard-size cupcakes

For the cupcakes

- 125 g (4¹/₂ oz) gluten-free flour
- 2 level tsp gluten-free baking powder
- 1 level tsp ground cinnamon
- 90 g (3 oz) butter, softened
- 4 Tbsp light brown soft sugar
- 1 dessert apple, cored and grated
- 2 medium eggs
- 2 Tbsp milk
- 150 g (5¹/₂ oz) dates, stoned and finely chopped

For the topping

- 3–4 level Tbsp demerara sugar

- *12-hole bun tray lined with paper cases*

1 Preheat the oven to 180° C/350° F (gas 4).

2 To make the cupcakes, sift the flour, baking powder and cinnamon into a bowl. Add the butter, sugar, apple, eggs and milk, and beat until smooth. Stir in the chopped dates. Spoon the mixture into the paper cases and level the surface.

3 For the topping, sprinkle the demerara sugar over the cupcakes. bake in the centre of the oven for 15 to 20 minutes until the cakes have risen and are just firm to the touch in the centre. Remove the cakes from the oven and transfer them to a wire rack to cool.

Blueberry and vanilla

Fruit sugar is a natural occuring sugar and is sweeter than regular sugar, so you don't have to add as much of it. Adding the blueberries also helps to sweeten the cakes.

Makes 12 standard-size cupcakes

For the cupcakes
- 100 (3½ oz) butter, softened
- 50 g (2 oz) fruit sugar
- 100 g (3½ oz) self-raising flour
- 2 medium eggs
- Few drops of vanilla extract
- 100 g (3½ oz) blueberries
- 30 g (1 oz) hazelnuts, roughly chopped

- *12-hole bun tray lined with paper cases*

1 Preheat the oven to 180° C/350° F (gas 4).

2 To make the cupcakes, place the butter, fruit sugar, flour, eggs and vanilla extract into a bowl, and beat until smooth. Stir in the blueberries. Divide the mixture between the paper cases and scatter the chopped nuts over the top. Bake in the centre of the oven for 12 to 15 minutes until the cakes have risen and are a light golden colour. Take care not to overcook them or the blueberries will break down and go mushy. Remove the cakes from the oven and transfer them to a wire rack.

> Freezing these cupcakes is not recommended, as the blueberries will become very soft once they have defrosted.

Ginger polenta

This doesn't look like a polenta recipe as the dark brown sugar disguises the yellow colour of the polenta.

Makes 12 standard-size cupcakes

For the cupcakes
- 125 g (4^1/$_2$ oz) butter, softened
- 125 g (4^1/$_2$ oz) dark brown sugar
- 1 Tbsp ground ginger
- Pinch salt
- 3 medium eggs
- 125 g (4^1/$_2$ oz) fine polenta
- 100 g (3^1/$_2$ oz) ground almonds
- 1 level tsp gluten-free baking powder
- 4 Tbsp milk

For the topping
- 6 pieces stem ginger in syrup
- 2–3 Tbsp ginger syrup (from stem ginger jar)

- *12-hole bun tray lined with paper cases*

1 Preheat the oven to 160° C/325° F (gas 3).

2 To make the cupcakes, beat the butter, sugar, ginger and salt together until light and fluffy, then beat in the eggs. Fold in the polenta, along with the ground almonds and baking powder. Spoon the mixture into the paper cases, levelling the surface of each. Bake in the centre of the oven for 15 to 20 minutes until the cakes have risen and are just firm to the touch in the centre. Remove the cakes from the oven and transfer them to a wire rack to cool.

3 For the topping, cut the stem ginger into long strips and scatter it over the cupcakes and spoon over some of the syrup.

Halloween webs

These cobweb-inspired cakes look pretty in contrasting colours. To make them easier and quicker to decorate, they could be decorated in just two colours.

Makes 12 standard-size cupcakes

For the cupcakes
- 125 g (4½ oz) butter, softened
- 125 g (4½ oz) caster sugar
- 2 medium eggs
- 2 Tbsp milk
- 125 g (4½ oz) gluten-free plain flour
- 1 level tsp gluten-free baking powder

For the topping
- 1 quantity of Thick glacé icing, see page 34
- 4 liquid or paste food colourings

- *12-hole bun tray lined with paper cases*
- *4 disposable piping bags*
- *Cocktail stick*

1 Preheat the oven to 190° C/375° F (gas 5).

2 To make the cupcakes, cream the butter and sugar together in a bowl until the mixture is light and fluffy. Add the eggs and milk, then sift over the flour and baking powder. Beat the mixture until smooth. Divide the mixture between the paper cases and bake in the centre of the oven for 12 to 15 minutes until the cakes have risen and are just firm to the touch in the centre. Remove the cakes from the oven and transfer them to a wire rack to cool.

3 For the topping, divide the glacé icing into four equal portions and take out 2 tablespoons from each portion. Colour each main portion in different colours and each smaller portion, which will be used for the webs, in contrasting colours. Working on one cake at a time, spread over the main

188

colour. Place the contrasting icing in a piping bag, cut off the tip and pipe a spiral over the icing. Pull a cocktail stick through the spiral from the centre out to give a feathered effect. Decorate three cupcakes of each colour combination.

Acknowledgements

**The author would like to thank the following companies
for supplying ingredients and equipment for the testing
of recipes and photography for this book. All these
companies offer a mail order service:**

Beryls
P.O. Box 1584
North Springfield
VA 22151
USA
www.beryls.com

Knightsbridge PME
Cake Decoration
Unit 9 & 10
Brember Road
South Harrow
Middlesex HA2 6AX
England
www.cakedecoration.co.uk

Squires Kitchen
Squires House
3 Waverley Lane
Farnham
Surrey GU9 8BB
England
www.squires-shop.com

Index